SPORT PARACHUTING

Charles W. Ryan

Henry Regnery Company · Chicago

Library of Congress Cataloging in Publication Data

Ryan, Charles W.
    Sport parachuting.

    Bibliography: p.
    Includes index.
    1. Parachuting. 2. Skydiving. I. Title.
GV770.R92   797.5'6   74-26687
ISBN 0-8092-8379-4
ISBN 0-8092-8378-6 pbk.

Illustrations on pages 112, 114 and 116
by T. E. Peiffer.

Copyright © 1975 by Charles W. Ryan
Published by Henry Regnery Company
    180 North Michigan Avenue
    Chicago, Illinois 60601
Manufactured in the United States of America
Library of Congress Catalog Card Number: 74-26687
International Standard Book Number: 0-8092-8379-4 (cloth)
                                    0-8092-8378-6 (paper)

Published simultaneously in Canada by
Fitzhenry & Whiteside Limited
150 Lesmill Road
Don Mills, Ontario M3B 2T5
Canada

To my friends in the
California Parachute Club
and in
the Diablo Skydivers

Contents

Preface

In the short span during which parachuting has been regarded as a sport, a number of books have appeared that, with rare exception, have made significant contributions to our young and growing activity—jumping out of airplanes for sport and pure enjoyment.

Now Chuck Ryan is responsible for another book on sport parachuting. To say he has authored the "complete" book of sport parachuting (or "skydiving") is perhaps going a little far, because the sport is constantly changing; new techniques, new equipment, and new ideas are being introduced practically on a month-to-month basis. Yet, it is my opinion that Chuck Ryan has come close to writing the complete book, and in this lies the greatest merit of his work.

This is not to say that one reading of the book will make you an instant skydiver—far from it, nor was this the author's intent. The book will prove a valuable reference and supplement for those who wish to become part of the beautiful world of freefall parachuting, always remembering, as the author notes throughout his work, there is never a substitute for good, sound, comprehensive training.

The book has value, too, for those who prefer to remain earthbound. You will become acquainted with the world of parachuting and its participants. Even more important, preconceived notions of our activity will be erased as you discover that what you thought to be wild and reckless abandon is really a serious and controlled approach to conquering one of man's alien environments. Then, perhaps, you will be able to grasp more completely the total beauty of this fantastic sport of ours.

Aviation, after many years of early struggle, has become firmly entrenched in, and an acceptable part of, our society. Parachuting also has been beset with struggles and uphill trudges over the years of our existence, but today it is an integral part of the aviation spectrum. In modern parachuting, as a complement to aviation, we recognize that innovations are a way of life. The pioneering spirit that characterized those early aviators leads us, too, to further improvement in our chosen activity.

It is this very spirit of pioneering, almost unique today, that enticed me into parachuting and, for 15 years, has continued to lure me to the drop zone. I am confident Chuck Ryan's book goes far toward capturing this feeling.

I hope so. It's a good feeling.

> Norman E. Heaton
> Executive Director
> United States Parachute Association

Introduction

When I made my first parachute jump, in 1967, I had no intention of getting into a new sport. In fact, my main question, a common one, about sport parachutists was: "Why would anyone want to jump out of a perfectly good airplane?"

However, I share with almost all writers an intense curiosity about the world I live in and a desire for new experiences, and for several years I had been intrigued by the idea of a parachute jump. Still my apprehension is revealed in the grammar of a statement I occasionally made about parachuting: "I would like *to have had* the experience of a parachute jump."

Anyway, I went through a stringent first-jump course at the Stevens School of Sport Parachuting in Oakland, California. But as I prepared to make that first jump at the California Parachute Club drop zone near Livermore, I still intended to make only a single jump. It didn't work out that way. By the time I landed, I was hooked on the sheer beauty of parachuting. Now, 1,100 jumps later, I still feel the same about the sport.

No one knows for sure just how many people in the United

States are active sport parachutists. A common estimate is about 30,000, almost 20,000 of whom belong to the United States Parachute Association. Part of the difficulty in an estimate is a definition of "active," but it is generally thought that two to three million parachute jumps are made each year in this country.

A little known and grossly misunderstood sport 10 years ago, parachuting has come of age. As public awareness of sport parachuting has increased, the old image of the "skydiver" as a thrill-seeking daredevil (probably with an innate death wish) has gradually faded. Parachutists come from an almost endless list of occupations: doctors, plumbers, architects, lawyers, tree surgeons, artists, firemen, housewives, bankers, secretaries, policemen, brokers, and probably a few burglars and confidence men. People who have almost nothing else in common share a love of the sport.

Both the technology of parachuting and the skill of parachutists have increased enormously over the past decade. National competitions are won by centimeters in accuracy and by fractions of a second in style. At the 1974 U.S. National Parachuting Championships, for instance, first and fourth places in style were separated by only 0.28 second, and there was a three-way tie for first place in accuracy, with three competitors scoring seven dead centers each and with each using a different type of parachute. (One of the parachutes was a prototype design that had not been marketed.)

Relative work, too, has matured. Not so many years ago, the passing of a baton in freefall was regarded as the epitome of relative work. In 1974, 31 parachutists linked hands in a huge falling circle.

No one can write a book about sport parachuting without the assistance and advice of many knowledgeable people. I am especially indebted to the many photographers whose pictures appear throughout the book. The cooperation of the United States Parachute Association has been invaluable, and thanks are due the many expert parachutists who reviewed all or portions of the manuscript and offered many helpful suggestions. To the extent that this book represents an accurate view of sport parachuting, those individuals share a major portion of the credit.

1

Historical Highlights

The idea of the parachute has been around for centuries. Leonardo da Vinci designed a parachute about 1495, and his Italian countryman Fouste Veranzio is said to have made an actual jump from a tower in Venice under a crude canvas parachute in 1617. (Historians are not sure this actually happened.) There was no real need for parachutes, however, until after the development of balloons in the 18th and 19th centuries and powered aircraft in the early 20th century. People then began to give serious thought to methods of safe escape from disabled air vehicles.

EARLY HISTORY

As early as 1783 men were experimenting with parachutes. It was then that the Montgolfier brothers of ballooning fame dropped a sheep from a high tower and watched it descend safely under a 7-foot chute. In the same year Sebastien Leormand claimed to have jumped from another high tower him-

1

self, under a 14-foot parachute. (The record is less than certain.) J. P. Blanchard supported his claim to a 1793 parachute jump with the story of a broken leg; though no solid proof of his jump exists, it does seem unlikely that a man falsely claiming the parachute jump would tarnish his glory with such a report.

Documentation does exist for parachute jumps made at the end of the 18th century. Parisian André Jacques Garnerin's successful 1797 jump from a balloon at 2,000 feet is fact. Garnerin, who is generally credited with being the first parachutist, also discovered a side effect of descents under his parachute—airsickness. Air spilling out under the edges of the parachute caused it to oscillate violently. The problem was solved by cutting a small hole in the apex, which allowed a steady escape route for air and greatly increased parachute stability. This hole in the apex became a standard design feature of later parachutes.

Other parachuting firsts include Jodaki Kuparento and Englishman Robert Cocking. Kuparento, who left his burning balloon over Warsaw in 1808 wearing a parachute, is credited with the parachute's first emergency use. And Cocking became the first known parachuting fatality when he fell to his death in 1837 during demonstration of what he thought was a parachute with a safer design.

EARLY 20TH-CENTURY DEVELOPMENT

Parachuting development really picked up speed in the early 20th century with the advent of powered flight. During World War I the policymakers of several nations began to think about parachutes for their pilots. And when crowds became bored with the crazy stunt fliers barnstorming at carnivals and fairs across the country, even crazier parachutists entered the picture and became an instant hit.

Georgia Thompson (Tiny) Broadwick was very much a part of the "show" scene in those early days. She began her 1,100-

Tiny Broadwick, about to take off in a "hydro-aeroplane," flown by Glenn Martin, for a jump into Lake Michigan in 1913. She released herself from the "trap seat" at 2000 feet. (USPA Photo)

jump career in 1908 when, at age 15, she jumped from a balloon over Raleigh, North Carolina. Mrs. Broadwick has long had recognition as the first woman to jump from an aircraft, but a lesser known fact is that she was the first *person* to make a freefall parachute jump. The latter honor is usually accorded to Leslie L. Irvin.

The story of Tiny's first freefall jump is an interesting one. All early parachutists used some device connected to the balloon or airplane—either the bag in which the parachute was stowed or a line called a static line—to open their parachutes as they fell away from the aircraft. In 1914, at North Island, San Diego, California, Tiny narrowly escaped a serious accident when her static line became tangled on the tail section of the airplane during a series of parachute demonstrations for the U.S. government (another first). To insure that her next and final jump would be accident-free, Tiny cut off the static line and pulled this makeshift ripcord after she was clear of the airplane and in *freefall*, becoming the first parachutist in history to make a freefall parachute jump.[1] It was not until five years later, on April 28, 1919, that Leslie Irvin made the freefall jump that has since gone into the record books as the first.

But Tiny Broadwick's jump is not the only freefall jump worth historical mention. On August 16, 1960, U.S. Air Force Captain Joseph W. Kittinger left a balloon at 102,800 feet over Tularosa, New Mexico, and fell for 4 minutes 38 seconds before his parachute opened at about 17,500 feet, to make the *longest* freefall jump. And the longest *first-jump* freefall is probably that of entertainer Johnny Carson, who jumped from 12,500 feet and fell for 60 seconds, on July 5, 1968. Bob Sinclair fell with Carson, holding his harness until Carson, who was equipped with an automatic opener, pulled his ripcord. Carson later ran the video tape of the event on his "Tonight Show."

Lieutenant Harold R. Harris is credited with the first freefall jump *in an actual emergency*. On October 22, 1922, Harris bailed out of his disabled airplane, fell 2,000 feet while fumbling for his ripcord, and finally got a parachute open at 500 feet. (Though pilots had been saved by parachutes in World War I, those parachutes were opened by static lines attached to the aircraft.) It is interesting to note that had Harris delayed three seconds longer in opening his chute, he would have provided a more tragic statistic, and the widespread use of emergency parachutes might have been delayed for many years.

A month after Harris's jump, the Caterpillar Club was formed. Each person who used his parachute to save his life in a true emergency received a small gold caterpillar pin to mark the event. Though pins are no longer awarded, people still call

---

1. After I submitted documentation of Mrs. Broadwick's historic freefall jump to Guinness Superlatives Limited, publishers of *Guinness Book of World Records*, Editor Norris D. McWhirter informed me that future editions of the book will list Georgia (Tiny) Broadwick as the first person to make a freefall parachute jump.

Johnny Carson (right) receives final equipment check by Bob Sinclair before making a single jump—a 60-second freefall from 12,500 feet—on July 5, 1968. (Photo Courtesy of Professional Parachutists)

themselves members of the Caterpillar Club when they meet that single requirement.

In addition to dramatic events, parachuting development depended on the disproving of long-held myths. One misconception was that the sudden shift in weight caused by a parachutist leaving a plane would make the aircraft go out of control; until this was proven incorrect, pilots were understandably reluctant to carry parachutists. Another early fear was that a parachutist would go hopelessly out of control on a long drop; indeed this can happen, but in 1925 Steven Budreau fell safely 3,500 feet over Selfridge Field, Michigan, proving stable freefall as a technique.

PRACTICAL USES

As false fears were laid to rest, practical parachuting expanded. In 1928, General Billy Mitchell had six men jump from a Martin bomber and, upon landing, set up a machine gun, demonstrating the potential usefulness of paratroopers. (The United States did not pursue this idea until Rotterdam was taken by German paratroopers in 1939; then the United States and its future allies became seriously interested in airborne training. The 82nd and 101st Airborne Divisions demonstrated the effectiveness of paratroopers in the invasion of Normandy on D Day, June 6, 1944.) In 1933 Russians proved the feasibility of mass jumping of parachutists when 62 parachutists jumped from three bombers. Military use of parachutes was further expanded in World War II when jeeps and other heavy equipment were dropped into combat zones.

Today, parachuting is employed in many practical ways. "Smoke jumpers," parachuting fire fighters, have become an effective weapon in the constant battle against forest fires.[2] Supplies and equipment—as well as food for people and animals—have been dropped by parachute into inaccessible or snowbound areas. Parachutists have also contributed to the scientific exploration of isolated areas, and paramedics have used their skills to save lives in areas where rapid access by land was impossible.

SPORT PARACHUTING

In the meantime, parachuting was also coming into its own as a sport. The Russians held the first sport parachuting competition at a Sports Festival in 1930. Amateur jumpers competed for accuracy in landing near a specified target. The United States followed suit in 1932 when 40 parachutists competed at the National Air Races at Roosevelt Field, New York.

As early as 1933, the Soviet Union had a national organization of sport parachutists that operated under government

---

2. The Forestry Service operates a smoke jumpers' school at Missoula, Montana. However, sport parachutists interested in this specialized parachuting activity need to be aware of two things. First, the Forestry Service prefers candidates with no jumping experience, because training is more effective if nothing has to be unlearned. Second, the parachute is mere transportation, and when the descent is in the vicinity of a burning forest, with winds made treacherous by fire, it is hazardous transportation at that. When the jump is over, unglamorous, backbreaking work is the smoke jumper's lot.

Joe Crane's efforts led to founding of the National Parachute Jumpers Association, a forerunner of the USPA. (USPA Photo)

subsidy. By 1949 France was subsidizing sport parachuting and had established several sport parachuting centers. Also in France sophisticated techniques of effective body control in freefall were developed, later to be brought to the United States by Jacques Istel.

This experimentation, by men such as Floyd Smith, Leo Valentin, and Jacques Istel, led to the origin of two other important areas of sport parachuting—style and relative work. Style consists of aerobatic maneuvers judged for speed and precision. In relative work, jumpers maneuver together to achieve freefall formations.

An early advocate of sport parachuting in the United States, Joe Crane, persuaded the National Aeronautic Association (NAA) to sanction all formal sport parachuting competitions in the United States and became the first official representative of sport parachuting when he joined the NAA Board of Directors. Crane led efforts to secure better contracts and conditions for the many professional parachutists who were performing at air shows and other public activities, and his pi-

Bob McDermott, First Sergeant of the Army Parachute Team. (Photo by Joe Gonzales)

oneering work led to the formation of the National Parachute Jumpers Association, which evolved into the National Parachute Jumpers and Riggers, Inc. (NPJR), in 1946. In 1957, NPJR became the Parachute Club of America (PCA), and, in 1967, the organization took its current name, the United States Parachute Association (USPA). Though never subsidized, sport parachuting gained greater impetus in the U.S. when the army, reversing an earlier attitude, began to encourage parachuting in 1958. The Strategic Army Corps Parachute Team, formed in 1959 at Fort Bragg, North Carolina, was renamed the U.S. Army Parachute Team two years later and adopted a nickname, "Golden Knights," in 1962.

Today the Army Parachute Team, currently numbering about 60 men, is organized into two demonstration units (which perform all over the United States and abroad), a competition team, a research and development section, an aviation section, and other support elements performing administrative, operations, supply, public information, and photographic duties. The competition unit has been in the forefront of competition in the United States ever since the team was formed and has distinguished itself in both national and international competition.

INTERNATIONAL COMPETITION

It was clear that sport parachuting had arrived as a recognized sport when five European nations met in Yugoslavia in 1951 for an international parachuting competition.

The Second World Parachuting Championships were held at St. Yan, France. Army Sergeant Fred Mason, then stationed in Europe, was the single American representative; he competed along with jumpers from eight other countries. International sport parachuting competition gained the recognition of the Federation Aeronautique Internationale (FAI) as a result of this meet, and FAI-sanctioned World Parachuting Championships have been held in each even-numbered year since 1954. (A summary of all World Parachuting Championships is presented in Appendix B.)

Fred T. Mason, the first American in international competition, was the lone U.S. representative at the Second World Parachuting Championships in St. Yan, France, 1954. (USPA Photo)

In 1956 the United States sent a team to the Third World Parachuting Championships in Moscow and finished sixth out of the 10 countries entered. The United States also participated as host country in 1962 and 1972. In odd-numbered years the Adriatic Cup is held in Portoroz, Yugoslavia. (It is unfeasible, both economically and as a matter of time, to hold a world competition every year.) Though this competition has been held eight times and thus has standing as a traditional competition, Americans generally regard it as less than a true test of parachuting skill. But, despite this attitude, and the distinct feeling that politically influenced judges are not exactly impartial, Americans generally attend the Adriatic Cup. One reason is that the team selected at the U.S. Nationals in odd-numbered years would have nowhere to go without the

Adriatic Cup. In 1973, the U.S. style and accuracy team made history at the Eighth Adriatic Cup by becoming the first Westerners to sweep this competition. Both American teams, men and women, ended up in first place.

A new competition, held only twice so far, is the Pan-American Cup. The Americans have dominated this competition, intended for countries in this hemisphere, both times, which is not surprising, since sport parachuting is relatively undeveloped in the Americas outside the United States and Canada.

Competition in sport parachuting is not without controversy. International parachuting competitions have become a means, in the view of some nations, of adding to national prestige, and in these countries sport parachuting is heavily subsidized. The United States government does not subsidize sport parachutists, even members of U.S. teams in international competition. Most other Western nations give little or no financial assistance to the parachutists who might bring home gold medals and national honor.

However, this lack of help from the U.S. government is not necessarily deplorable. Americans compete for the love of the sport, sometimes even risking personal bankruptcy to win a place on a U.S. Parachute Team. And they seem to be holding their own against the totally subsidized Soviets, whom the Americans look upon as the parachutists to beat. This competition is not purely political; many of the world's best sport parachutists live in the Soviet Union.

RELATIVE WORK

The international competitions mentioned so far have been concerned only with style and accuracy, the two traditional categories of competition. The third category, relative work, has been somewhat neglected until the past few years. (The Adriatic Cup does include a baton pass in one event, but this no longer qualifies as a demonstration of relative work skill.)

World record 31-man star over Elsinore, California on August 4, 1974. (Photo by M. Anderson Jenkins)

Relative work, encompassing anything beyond a simple baton pass, was born and nourished in the United States, particularly in California. However, the first baton pass, although accomplished by Americans, took place in Vancouver, British Columbia. In the early summer of 1958 Lyle Hoffman and James Pearson, both of the Seattle Skydivers, managed to pass a baton in freefall. A month later, on July 16, 1958, the feat was repeated by Steve Snyder and Charlie Hillard over Fort Bragg, North Carolina.

Little by little, parachutists learned to maneuver together in freefall. They learned to form "stars," circles of parachutists holding hands while falling, a much more complicated exercise than passing a baton. With each additional person the difficulty of forming a star increased, because of the delicate balance and maneuvering required to maintain the formation. And with the amount of safe freefall time another governing factor, speed had to be developed as well as finesse.

Six years after the first baton pass, on September 6, 1964, six parachutists managed to form a six-man star over Arvin, California. The jumpers piled out of two aircraft at 12,000 feet and formed the star in about 30 seconds. A year later the Arvin Good Guys formed the world's first eight-man star. In June 1967 the record star reached 10 over Taft, California. A week later another group duplicated the feat over Elsinore, California, and in November of the same year a 10-man star competition was held, with the winning team putting together back-to-back 10-man stars. The race to form larger and larger stars continues. The current record stands at 31 (at Elsinore, California, in August 1974), but that number could be surpassed at any time.

Sequential relative work, performing more than one formation in succession, is another relative work development. A four-man relative work event was included in the U.S. National Parachuting Championships in 1970, at Plattsburg, New York. Two years later, in Tahlequah, Oklahoma, a 10-man event was added to the competition. The four-man teams perform sequential relative work, while the 10-man teams try to complete 10-man stars in the shortest possible time. The world record for completion of a 10-man star, as this is written, is 12.76 seconds—a feat accomplished in August 1974 by the Wings of Orange team captained by Jerry Bird.

With 31-man stars, style events and regular world championships, sport parachuting has come a long way since the Russian factory workers held an accuracy contest in 1930. Today, through the efforts of the FAI, the organization of sport parachuting is worldwide, although most parachuting activity naturally centers in the countries that are more technologically advanced. And it is not without reason that many call sport parachuting "the sport of the space age."

Student approaches target under a conventional canopy with a TU modification. (Photo by Terry Schumacher)

2

Getting Started

Once you decide to make your first parachute jump, whether for the once-only experience or for the beginning of an exciting and challenging sport, several questions immediately occur to you.

One of these may be, "Can I go through with it?" The answer to this one is a definite "Yes!" Of those who enter a first jump course, a very small percentage voluntarily drop out, but it is almost a certainty that if you show up at the drop zone and external conditions such as weather permit it, you will make the jump. A refusal to jump the first time is so rare that most Jumpmasters have never experienced this situation. (A student might refuse to leave the aircraft on a later jump, but almost never on the first one.)

So, if you think the experience of a parachute jump is for you, you need the answers to these three questions:

- Where can I jump?
- How much will it cost?
- What is the training like?

WHERE TO JUMP

Parachuting, despite the quality of "adventure" inherent in the sport, is strictly controlled, not only by federal and (in some cases) state regulation but by the hard facts of safety and economics.

In the early years of sport parachuting, commercial centers were all but nonexistent, because the amount of activity was not attractive as a business venture. Clubs were formed because they were the only practical means to deal with the necessities of jumping—finding a location and arranging for an airplane to take the jumpers up.

Later, as sport parachuting attracted ever increasing numbers of enthusiasts, commercial centers were established in response to the basic law of business: "Find a need and fill it."

In the United States today there are about 250 active clubs and perhaps 50 commercial parachuting centers. An up-to-date list of clubs and commercial centers is provided in Chapter 6. Clubs are found in most of the 50 states. The commercial centers listed range from giants, such as the Parachutes Incorporated centers in Orange, Massachusetts, and Lakewood, New Jersey, to small operations that train only a few students each week.

If you want to get into sport parachuting, the *only* way is to contact a club or commercial center—or a school of sport parachuting associated with a club or commercial drop zone. Any other procedure is unsafe, impractical, and probably illegal.

If you live in or near a metropolitan area, there is probably a commercial center near you, but the drop zone will be located far from the heart of the city, since there must be space to land.

In most areas, you can probably find one or more clubs

Parachutes Incorporated drop zone at Orange, Massachusetts. (Photo by Joe Gonzales)

within a 100-mile radius. Of course, if you live in a state such as California, Texas, or Florida, where good weather permits year-round jumping, you are likely to find several clubs within easy reach. While clubs are not likely to be listed in the yellow pages of your telephone book, commercial centers often are. Local Federal Aviation Administration (FAA) offices will often have information about drop zones in your vicinity.

THE COST

The cost of a first jump varies in different regions and with different arrangements for instruction, equipment, insurance, and the airplane ride, but you can safely figure that it will fall within a range of about $50 to $75. You can expect to pay more at a commercial center, but in many cases, you also get more for your money.

One of the largest operators of commercial centers in the country, Parachutes Incorporated, has centers at Orange, Massachusetts (founded in 1967, it is the oldest in the country), Lakewood, New Jersey, and Crawfordsville, Indiana. The Sixth World Parachuting Championships, with 25 nations competing, were held in Orange in 1962. Although the PI centers are larger than most, they are fairly typical of the larger commercial operations.

The total cost of a first jump at PI centers includes *everything* you need for a first jump. If you are in good health, at least 16 years old (with parents' consent) or have reached legal majority, and if you have the fee, you can receive your training and make your first jump on the same day. The basic fee pays for:

- classroom instruction
- practical training, such as parachute landing falls and emergency procedures
- boots, coveralls, and helmet
- main and reserve parachutes, inspected and packed by a licensed rigger
- the airplane ride to 2,800 feet, the altitude from which you will make your first jump
- supervision of your jump by a professional jumpmaster
- liability insurance

Note that the last item is *liability* insurance. This does not cover injury to yourself or damage to your own gear. It *does* cover personal and property damage to others resulting from your parachuting activity. You will not be allowed to jump at most drop zones without liability insurance. Parachutes Incorporated has its own insurance plans, which are also available at a number of other commercial centers throughout the country that are not otherwise affiliated with that company. Many commercial centers, however, provide liability insurance coverage by requiring that you join the United States Parachute Association before you jump; the cost of membership in USPA is included in the fee for your first jump course. The USPA insurance, carried through Lloyd's of London, has limits of $5,000 property damage, $10,000 personal injury, or $20,000 per incident.

Your second jump at PI centers costs under $20, less if it is made on the same day as your first. Or you can buy a four-jump package for less than $60. The jump price includes *all* your equipment and the packing of your parachute. If, after a few jumps, you have learned to pack your own main parachute, you can save the repack charge.

Typical of the moderately sized commercial centers is the Antioch Sport Parachute Center at Antioch, California. The price of a first jump is a little less than that at the larger PI centers. Antioch, like Parachutes Incorporated, has its own insurance and provides the same training and parachute-rigging facilities. It charges slightly less than PI centers for second and subsequent jumps. The time required to complete the first jump course, however, is several hours longer than that at the PI centers. In my opinion, this is a definite advantage to the student.

An important difference at Antioch is a very thorough course in packing the main parachute. You must take this course after your second jump. You are not allowed to go on with further jumps until you have passed the course.

The packing course includes information about the construction and nomenclature of the parachute, harness, and container, practice in clearing tangled lines, and closely supervised packing of about 15 main parachutes. When you have demonstrated the ability to pack the main parachute, you continue with your jumping.

At this point you are in the "first freefall course," which takes you through your remaining static line jumps (usually three) and the first freefall, on which you pull your own ripcord. The cost of this instruction is in addition to the regular jump fee, which includes the equipment, airplane ride, and Jumpmaster.

At both Orange and Antioch, as well as at most other commercial centers, you reach a point, usually on 20-second delays, at which you no longer need a Jumpmaster. After that, you have to provide all your own equipment, either through rental or purchase, and the cost of your jump drops to the standard rate, which varies with altitude from about $4 to $5 for 3,000 feet to about $8 to $10 for 12,500 feet.

Since you will probably want to make several jumps before you decide to invest in your own equipment, almost all commercial centers rent equipment to you. Some typical prices for the rental of necessary equipment are:

- main parachute, about $15 to $20 per month
- reserve parachute, $1 to $2 per jump
- boots, helmet, and jump suit, $.50 to $2 per item per day

If you receive your first jump training at a club rather than at a commercial center, your cost for the first jump will range from about $50 to $75, depending on so many variables that an itemization is impossible. You will probably have to join the United States Parachute Association before your first jump, but this is offset by a lower typical fee for the ground training. Clubs are nonprofit operations, but they still pay their Instructors to train new students.

A student program is important to any club because it is the only way to bring new life into the club as members move away or drop out of sport parachuting. If you start jumping with a club instead of a commercial center, there are some decided advantages for you. You feel part of an organization, associate with more experienced jumpers from the beginning, and generally get more personalized supervision.

One disadvantage in many clubs is that you may have to wait longer for your jumps. Clubs generally do not have as many airplanes as commercial centers, so you may have to wait for a while to get a place on a jump load. On the whole, however, your jumping activities depend mostly on your own initiative and your pocketbook, whether you jump with a club or with a commercial center.

While the first jump may cost as much or more at a club, subsequent jumps usually cost far less. Typical is the oldest club in the country, the California Parachute Club at Livermore, California. *Each* student jump costs the same—$6—as long as you need a Jumpmaster. (In addition, you will pay a manifest fee of $.50 for the first jump of the day, just like everyone else, student or licensed jumper.) This fee covers your airplane ride, the services of your Jumpmaster, and $1 for the reserve parachute.

Clubs generally furnish all equipment for the first jump, but you must very quickly arrange for your own gear, usually through rental, after that. But because it is a club, rather than a commercial operation, you will find that there are many people willing to help you acquire gear and get on with the sport.

THE TRAINING

There is a lot of anxiety associated with sport parachuting, so you should start out, for your own peace of mind, by assuring yourself that your training is adequate for a safe first jump.

The first thing you can and should do is to check credentials. The United States Parachute Association has enormous influence on sport parachuting in the United States, and most jumpers belong to, or at least respect the standards of, that organization.

When you contact a club or a commercial center to inquire about the first jump training, don't just ask something like, "Do you follow the recommendations and standards of the United States Parachute Association?" You are not going to get "no" for an answer. (Actually, the "yes" answer is truthful in most cases anyway.)

The important things to consider are (1) what kind of training will you receive and (2) who is going to train you. The

First jump student makes a beautiful exit, but he closed his eyes. (Photo by Bob Cowan)

Basic Safety Regulations of the USPA require that only USPA-rated Instructors conduct the first jump training. So start out by asking to see the rating. My own Instructor rating, with photograph and current validation, is pictured in this chapter.

UNITED STATES PARACHUTE ASSOCIATION
INSTRUCTOR RATING

NAME __CHARLES W. RYAN__ US/FAI __D-2399__

ADDRESS __1257 Surf Ave., Pacific Grove, CA 93950__

D. O. B.	Height	Weight
14 Dec 29	5-9	155

Hair	Eyes	Sex	Date of Issue
Brn	Blue	M	12-20-70

The above individual has fulfilled all the requirements as set forth by the United States Parachute Association and the National Aeronautic Association and is certified as a USPA Instructor.

CERTIFYING USPA OFFICIAL

SIGNATURE OF INSTRUCTOR

ANNUAL RENEWAL

This rating is valid only when the card bears the official USPA Seal and the proper renewal stamp. This card must be returned to the USPA for annual renewal together with verification of minimum renewal requirements (see reverse side for Annual Renewal Requirements).

VALID 1971 U.S.P.A.	VALID THRU DECEMBER 1972	VALID THRU DECEMBER 1973	VALID THRU DECEMBER 1974

The author's USPA Instructor rating.

The only way to get an Instructor rating is through an Instructor Certification Course, the means by which the candidate demonstrates proficiency in teaching and a knowledge of the fundamentals of safe sport parachuting. He must have received his Jumpmaster rating, won through a difficult program of training and demonstration of proficiency, at least a year before he attends the Instructor Certification Course, so if your trainer can produce the Instructor rating, you can assume that you are in good hands. If he cannot, look elsewhere for your first jump training.

The length of the first jump course varies from about 3 hours in some clubs and commercial centers to a full weekend, with the average about 6 to 8 hours. An adequate length of time is difficult to state definitely, because the number of students going through training and the amount of personal instruction enter into the equation. (My own feeling, not supported by reliable statistics, is that 3 hours is not enough for the student to absorb the emergency procedures and other elements of training.)

The first jump course includes, but may not be limited to:

- aircraft exits
- stable position and ripcord pull
- emergency procedures
- canopy manipulation
- parachute landing falls

In addition, you will receive some familiarization instruction about the parachute equipment, you will probably see a film about sport parachuting, and you may receive some instruction in parachute packing. Although first jump instruction is outlined in the following paragraphs, details—such as *how* to make a good parachute landing fall or *how* to make a stable exit from an airplane—are not included. These techniques cannot be reliably taught in a book. The supervision of a competent Instructor during ground training and a competent Jumpmaster on the actual jump is an essential aspect of your introduction to sport parachuting.

Aircraft Exits

You will receive training in aircraft exits either in a mock-up of the jump aircraft or in an actual airplane on the ground. You will be taught how to sit in the aircraft on the ride up, and you will practice climbing out and making the exit from the aircraft.

Student practices exit from Cessna 182 jump aircraft. (Photo by James Kirk)

Stable Position and Ripcord Pull

A stable, face-to-earth falling position is mandatory not only for successful maneuvers on your student jumps but for your safety. If your parachute opens while you are falling with your back to earth, a malfunction is more likely. Thus, much of your first jump training is designed to teach you to fall in a stable position. This includes a hard arch, with your head up and your arms and legs in a spread-eagle position, to insure that you fall face to earth.

The count is part of the stability drill and is designed to take you through the ripcord pull and lead you into your emergency procedures if this becomes necessary. Here is the standard count:

- "One thousand." You maintain the hard arch.
- "Two thousand." You look at your dummy ripcord.
- "Three thousand." You pull the dummy ripcord.
- "Four thousand." You return your arms to standard stable position.
- "Five thousand." You maintain the stable position.
- "Six thousand." If you have not felt an opening shock,

Student practices arch and count. (Photo by James Kirk)

Cadet parachutists at the U.S. Air Force Academy use the suspended harness for training in canopy control, reserve activation, and preparation for landing. (USAFA photo)

you throw away the main ripcord, bend at the waist with your hand over your reserve ripcord handle, and look over your shoulder. If you see nothing coming out of the parachute pack, you pull the reserve.

Emergency Procedures

You can see that this subject is not entirely separate but pervades all your training. After the count of "six thousand" mentioned above, you are already into the emergency procedure for the total malfunction (nothing is coming out of the pack).

Actually, a pilot chute hesitation, in which nothing is wrong with your opening but the pilot chute has not yet "caught air," is a common occurrence. When you bend over the reserve, the flow of air around your body is changed, and a normal opening occurs.

Your training in emergency procedures includes instruction and practice. All emergency procedures in the air are related to some failure of the main parachute. Either nothing comes out (total malfunction), or the parachute opens but something is wrong with it (partial malfunction).

The two main types of partial malfunction are the "line over," in which one or more lines are over the top of your canopy when it opens, or a streamer, in which the canopy material is clinging together without allowing air inside to inflate it.

You are taught to recognize all types of malfunctions and to follow the proper procedure for dealing with each.

The practical portion of this training is accomplished in a suspended harness, simulating your position under the malfunctioned parachute. (If there is no suspended harness available for your first jump training, go elsewhere. Emergency procedures cannot be taught adequately without the suspended harness.)

Canopy Manipulation

All sport parachutes have "modifications" cut into the canopy to give the parachute forward speed and maneuverability through the use of steering lines (sometimes called toggle lines). Your instruction will include the technical details of how the canopy moves over the ground (a student canopy has a forward speed of about 4 to 8 mph) and how you will use this information to guide your canopy to a safe landing.

While you will not choose your own exit point for the first few jumps (your Jumpmaster does this), you will learn how the wind drift indicator is used to determine the winds aloft and, thus, the exit point.

Steering the conventional parachute. (Photo by Charles Dieter)

The wind drift indicator is a long, crepe paper streamer weighted to provide the same rate of descent as an open canopy.

It is not intended that you will make a precision landing on your first jump, but you do need to know enough about canopy control to maneuver your parachute around or away from obstacles and to a safe landing location.

Your training in canopy manipulation will include both classroom instruction and practice in the suspended harness.

Parachute Landing Falls

Drill in parachute landing falls (PLF's) is an important part of your first jump training because without this drill, you are very likely to suffer a sprain or a broken bone on landing. A

Student lands a bit off the target, but safety comes first—precision, later. (Photo by James Kirk)

Training in parachute landing falls (PLFs) at the U.S. Air Force Academy. (USAFA photo)

good portion of your time during first jump training is allocated to make sure you land safely.

This drill, conducted from a platform 3 or 4 feet high onto a padded mat or sawdust pit, continues until you can correctly accomplish the PLF. If you can't do a good PLF, you will not be allowed to jump.

When you land, you must distribute the force over other parts of your body and away from your feet and ankles. The

PLF allows your body to accept the shock at five points: feet, calf, thigh, buttocks, and shoulder.

The PLF drill brings unused muscles into play, so don't be surprised if you have trouble getting out of bed the next morning after this drill!

In addition to the basics, you also learn how to "field pack" your parachute for bringing it back to the packing area (in case your canopy control is not as good as it should be), and you learn the routine to be followed at the drop zone.

The First Jump

When you go out to the drop zone to make your first jump, all your training will fall into place, so don't worry about it. If you are not ready, you will not be allowed to jump.

When it is time to "chute up" for your jump, your Jumpmaster will give you an equipment check, adjust your harness for comfort and safety, and review your emergency procedures.

If you are equipped with a radio, for more positive ground control, you will be taught how to respond to radioed instructions. The USPA recommends that your reserve parachute be equipped with an automatic opener. If you have one, you will be briefed on its operation.

Jumpmaster completes equipment check of first-jump student. Both will don helmets before boarding aircraft. (photo by James Kirk)

Student receives
critique after
jump. (Photo by
James Kirk)

The automatic opener is a backup device that will open the reserve parachute at about 1,000 feet, if you do not have an opening of the main parachute by that time. With the newer models, there is nothing for you, the student, to do except to draw comfort from the fact that it is there. If you have an older model, you will have to turn it off after the parachute opens, and your Jumpmaster will have shown you how.

From the time the airplane leaves the ground until you leave the airplane, you are completely under the supervision and control of the Jumpmaster. Your safety is literally in his hands.

The Jumpmaster is well aware of this awesome responsibility, and you can be sure that he has your safety in mind at every moment. You must have complete confidence in your Jumpmaster. If you do not, don't jump.

After the First Jump

You are not abandoned after your first jump. You are a student until you receive a USPA license, which means that you will be supervised throughout the student program.

Chapter 3 will give you a good idea of what happens after the first jump.

Jumpmaster completes equipment check and briefing of student as experienced jumpers wait to load. (Photo by James Kirk)

3

Student Program

The USPA defines a "student" as someone who has not made a parachute jump but is in training for one, while a person who has made at least one jump but is not licensed is a "novice." In general practice (and in this book), however, the term, "novice," is little used. You are known as a student until you are licensed.

After a minimum of five static line jumps, required by the Basic Safety Regulations, you may go to freefall. But notice that the key word is *minimum*. If you cannot perform properly on the static line jumps, you will not be allowed to progress to freefall, during which you pull your own ripcord.

The purpose of the static line jumps is to create a behavior pattern in your mind so that you may safely pull your own ripcord. That purpose is secondary, of course, to the main reason for the initial static line jumps, which is to make sure you get a parachute open, even if you panic.

You must, during your static line jumps, demonstrate the ability to pull a ripcord by pulling the *dummy* ripcord (a rip-

35

cord handle, without the cable), which is fitted into the rip-cord handle pocket on your harness. You must correctly pull the dummy ripcord on three successive jumps before you are allowed to go to freefall.

In addition, the last static line jump must be made on the same day as the first freefall.

Before you go to freefall, your parachute is opened by the static line, a length of very strong nylon webbing that is connected to a ring inside the airplane. This line, which is about 8 to 15 feet long, automatically pulls the pins of your container (or breaks the break-cord), allowing your parachute to open when the line becomes taut.

Your progress toward the license is marked by longer and

Jumpmaster briefs static-line students at California Parachute Club, Livermore, California. (Photo by Mark Solomon)

longer delays, usually with a minimum of three delays at each level, during which you gradually learn freefall maneuvers. Here is a typical progression:

- *First freefall.* From 3,200 feet above ground level (actually the altitude for 5-second delays).
- *Five-second delay from 3,200 feet.* You do nothing but fall stable.
- *Ten-second delay from 3,600 feet.* A longer stable delay with no other maneuvers.
- *Fifteen-second delay from 4,500 feet.* You learn to assume the "frog" position used by experienced jumpers and make 180-degree turns.
- *Twenty-second delay from 5,500 feet.* You turn to face the target and make 360-degree turns.
- *Thirty-second delay from 7,200 feet.* In a typical program, you might perform both a back loop and a barrel roll on your first jump at this altitude; on your second, slowly assume the body position for "tracking" (moving horizontally over the ground while in freefall), then practice getting in and out of the "track" position; and then, on the third jump at this altitude, you might just bomb out the door without an engine cut and practice tracking. What is actually expected of you on jumps at this altitude varies tremendously.

You don't actually have to do everything described here for your A license. USPA requirements call for three 30-second delays. No specific maneuvers are required except for demonstration of the ability to hold a heading in freefall and the performance of 360-degree flat turns to the right and left—and both of these requirements are usually met before you even get to 30-second delays.

Please note, however, that you will not be permitted to start learning relative work (during which you are in the air with at least one other person) until you have learned to track, because it is absolutely essential for safety that parachutists be able to move over the ground *away from each other* to get enough separation to open their parachutes safely without collision or entanglement with another jumper.

During your entire student career, from your first jump until you are licensed, you will be under the supervision of a Jumpmaster. The man or woman who jumpmasters you is totally responsible for your safety and is well aware of this awesome responsibility.

If the person who jumpmasters you has the USPA Jumpmaster rating, you can be sure he has gone through a rigorous program of training and is competent to supervise every aspect of your jump.

You will probably jump with many different Jumpmasters during your student career, each with his own personality and his own way of helping you solve any problems that may arise, but they all have one thing in common: a real concern for your safety.

Your Jumpmaster's responsibility begins with the equipment check. He must be sure that the equipment is safe and that you are wearing it properly. Once he is sure you are safely "chuted up," he will review your emergency procedures with you, correcting any mistakes you may make.

If you are still on the static line, he will have you go through your arch and count, leading into the emergency procedures. If you are on a higher delay, he might want to refresh your memory of the particular maneuvers you intend to perform.

The Jumpmaster will know what your performance has been in the past and what your particular problems are, because each of your jumps is logged in your own logbook, and remarks about each jump are entered by your Jumpmaster, both for your own information and for the guidance of those who may jumpmaster you on later jumps.

The logbook is your record of jumps for license and other requirements, but it is also a record of your progress. You will not be allowed to progress to a higher delay until you have demonstrated satisfactory performance of the maneuvers required at the lower delay.

Jumpmaster signs
student's logbook.
(Photo by Ron
Tavalero)

After your equipment check, briefing, and review of emergency procedures, you are ready for the jump whenever an aircraft is available. You are assigned to an aircraft by a manifester. Depending on circumstances, you might be the only student among experienced jumpers, or your Jumpmaster might be the only experienced jumper among a group of students.

Once the Jumpmaster has supervised your getting settled in the aircraft, you are ready to climb to altitude for the jump. You might be admiring the view, trying to deal with your anxieties, or going over the jump in your mind, but the *Jumpmaster* is busy with a number of things.

First, he is keeping an eye on every student to make sure no one does anything unsafe, such as allowing a reserve ripcord handle to snag on something. At the same time, he is directing the pilot on the jump run, having selected the point at which he wants you to leave the aircraft.

As the aircraft approaches the exit point, he gets you in posi-

Student exits over Ripcord West Sport Parachute Center, near St. Louis, Missouri, as the Jumpmaster observes. (photo by Bob Cowan)

tion to get out of the aircraft, calls for an engine cut (to reduce the wind blast), gives you the command to get out on the wheel or strut (or in the door; it depends on the aircraft), and gives you the command to go. The commands to get ready, get out of the airplane, and go are both verbal and physical—a slap on the shoulder to get out; a slap on the thigh to go. There will be no doubt what is expected of you, and when.

After you leave the plane, the Jumpmaster continues to observe you until your parachute is open so that he can tell you exactly what you did wrong (or right) when he critiques you after the jump. Another of the Jumpmaster's responsibilities, before the airplane takes off, is to be sure someone is on the ground to observe your descent and give you instructions if necessary.

As soon as possible after your jump, the Jumpmaster will discuss your jump with you. If you did something wrong or had a problem with the planned maneuvers, he will advise you so that you can correct your mistakes on the next jump. If you did nothing wrong (and this is often the case), he will also tell you that.

One of the great pleasures of your student career can be the camaraderie you develop with your Jumpmasters and the other students. But sometimes the rapport is not there, even though you may be a good student and your Jumpmaster outstanding. If you don't feel comfortable with a Jumpmaster, don't jump with him. You have plenty to think about without the added burden of personalities that don't mesh. The Jumpmaster's ego may be bruised, but he will probably understand.

During your early jumps, you will also be learning how to pack your own parachute. After your initial instruction, you will be closely supervised until someone with the authority to do so is satisfied that you can safely pack your parachute. After that, you are free to pack without supervision.

That is the *main* parachute, of course. *All* jumpers have to have the reserve parachute inspected and repacked by an FAA-certificated rigger within 60 days of any jump. (A change

Freefall student has just pulled his ripcord, and the parachute is starting to open. (USPA photo by William Kiehl)

to a 120-day repack cycle is currently being considered by the FAA.)

After 25 freefalls, including three good 30-second delays, and after you meet certain other requirements, such as the performance of certain maneuvers and the passing of a written examination, you may apply for the first license, the A license.

Possession of the A (or higher) license entitles you to jump without supervision at most drop zones. You are eligible for licensing, basically, when you have demonstrated that you can safely jump without supervision.

Once you are licensed, you are on your way. As you develop skill and experience, you may acquire higher licenses—the B, C, and D—each of which may be required for some particular rating or sport parachuting activity. These licenses are discussed in Appendix A.

4

Emergency Procedures

Many sport parachutists are fond of telling non-jumpers that the most dangerous part of parachuting is the drive to the airport. This is an exaggeration, but it does make a point. Parachuting is a lot safer than most people think; but this is true because we know there are hazards associated with the sport, and over the years, we have carefully developed standards of safety and drilled our students in proper emergency procedures.

There are about 40 parachuting fatalities in the United

Facing page. This rare photo sequence of a reserve opening at terminal velocity (120 mph) was captured in the days when most jumpers used reserves without pilot chutes, to avoid entanglement with the main parachute during manual deployment of the reserve without breakaway from the main. Top: Jumper pulls reserve ripcord. A back-to-earth position would have allowed the canopy to inflate without the obstruction of the jumper's body. Center: Reserve canopy catches air and blows past jumper's body. Bottom: As line stretch is reached when the canopy is fully inflated, jumper is pulled over on his back. (Photos by Ralph White)

45

States each year, in the course of an estimated two million parachute jumps made. Thus, if these figures are accurate, 0.002 percent of the jumps made each year end in death. But remember, that percentage includes *all* jumpers; those who observe safety procedures and those who do not. It includes students who make a first jump after the so-called quickie course and those who are drilled on emergency procedures until those procedures become second nature.

The safest course to follow in your parachuting career, if you jump, or if you intend to, is to learn the emergency procedures thoroughly and to review them often, remembering that we all, regardless of the number of jumps, subject ourselves to a certain degree of risk when we jump from an airplane.

A few parachuting deaths are caused by drowning, electrocution on power lines, or freakish circumstances; but most emergencies begin with the failure of a parachute to function properly. That is why federal law, the Basic Safety Regulations of the USPA, and common sense all require that the parachutist leave the airplane with two parachutes—his main, which he normally packs himself, and the auxiliary (reserve) parachute, which may be packed only by an FAA-certificated rigger.

The fact that parachutes sometimes malfunction is the reason emergency procedures taught all students deal mostly with what to do in case of a malfunction.

If a parachutist has been falling for at least 12 seconds when he pulls his ripcord at the legal altitude of 2,000 to 2,500 feet, depending on his license, he is 11 to 14 seconds from the ground if he remains in freefall; that is, if his parachute fails to open and he does nothing.

One reason for doing nothing is panic. Because parachutists (usually students on an early jump) can panic, automatic openers, calibrated to activate the reserve (or sometimes the main) parachute at 1,000 feet are recommended by the USPA.

Provided the parachutist does not panic, and he is not likely to do so if he is well trained or has jumped several times, that few seconds, though it seems to be a very short time, is sufficient for a jumper to do anything he needs to save himself.

There are two classes of main parachute malfunctions: partial and total.

PARTIAL MALFUNCTIONS

A partial malfunction of the parachute is one in which the parachute comes out of the container but does not properly deploy. The canopy may not inflate at all (this is called a *streamer*), the canopy may inflate but have some lines over it (*lineover* or "*Mae West*"), or the parachute may partially inflate or have something else wrong with it.

Most partial malfunctions are caused by an error in packing or by poor body position during the opening sequence. No one knows for sure what causes a streamer, however.

The USPA recommends two separate procedures for dealing with a partial malfunction. In order of preference, they are (1) the breakaway and (2) manually controlled deployment of the reserve parachute.

Breakaway

The breakaway (also called "cutaway") is a procedure by which the main canopy is released before the reserve parachute is opened. All sport parachute harnesses generally used in the United States have devices called canopy releases to which the parachute risers are connected. The parachute is securely attached to these releases, the most common of which are called Capewells, but they may be simply and quickly released if the parachutist desires to jettison the main canopy.

Once you have recognized a malfunction and an attempt to clear the malfunction has failed (you should not waste much time trying to clear it), the USPA recommends the following procedure:

    1.   Throw away the main ripcord. The ripcord cable

could entangle with the deploying reserve canopy, creating a "double malfunction."

2. Remove safety covers from both riser releases (Capewell cable releases only) and *look at the reserve handle.*

3. Assume the proper body position and activate the riser releases at the same time. Be sure to keep your eyes on the reserve handle during breakaway.

4. After breakaway from the main canopy, immediately attempt to pull the reserve ripcord handle manually, *even if the Stevens Cutaway System is used.* (The reserve static line is intended as a *backup* system. There is no record of its failure, but it is a mechanical device, and you must depend on *your own efforts*, not on some backup device.) Actually, no student using the Stevens Cutaway System has ever managed to pull the handle before the reserve static line does it for him, and the reserve canopy is fully inflated within about 100 feet after breakaway from the main.

Students should use the breakaway procedure only if they are equipped with a *reserve static line.* The only such system currently in use is the Stevens Cutaway System, and it is highly recommended. This system is merely a line that is attached to one of the main risers, properly secured and routed along the harness, and attached to the reserve ripcord handle. It in no way interferes with manual operation of the reserve. When the parachutist breaks away, he falls only a few feet away from the jettisoned main canopy, and then the reserve static line becomes taut, automatically pulling the reserve ripcord handle. Full inflation of the reserve usually occurs with a loss of altitude of no more than 100 to 150 feet. It is now used at about half the drop zones in the United States, and its use has spread rapidly since it was introduced in 1970.

If the breakaway procedure is used, *a pilot chute must be used in the reserve* for positive and immediate deployment.

Since two general types of reserves are in use, the chest- or front-mounted reserve and the piggyback (located on the back above the main parachute), the jumper must assume the best body position for allowing the reserve canopy to deploy freely.

Manually Controlled Procedure

The other method of reserve deployment is preferred by many parachutists because they believe that "something is better than nothing." The *something* is the main parachute, which—although it is not properly open—at least slows down your falling speed (unless the malfunction is a streamer). This gives you a little more time to get your reserve parachute inflated, and if the reserve does not open properly, the landing might do no more than injure you.

One thing wrong with the "something is better than nothing" theory is that a common malfunction of the standard parachute used by students is the lineover; and those nylon suspension lines, sawing across the nylon canopy, can cause the canopy to come apart, in which case the "something" becomes nothing, and you are in bad trouble.

If you decide to use the manually controlled procedure, *you must not have a pilot chute in the reserve*, because the pilot chute greatly increases the chance that the reserve will entangle with the main, leaving you with "garbage," and very likely you will suffer serious injury or death.

The manually controlled procedure is quite a bit more complicated than the breakaway. Once you have made the decision to deploy the reserve, the USPA recommends the following procedure:

1. Throw away the main ripcord.
2. Cross your legs to keep out the reserve canopy and suspension lines.
3. Place your left hand over the ripcord protector flap of the reserve, palm toward your stomach and thumb up.

4. Pull the reserve ripcord with the right hand and *throw it away.* (Many reserves now in use have a center pull rather than a right-hand pull, so you can use either hand.)
5. Roll the left hand (the hand covering the ripcord protector flap) outward, allowing the reserve container to open while still retaining the canopy in the container.
6. Place the right hand (hand used to pull the reserve ripcord handle) under the top flap of the reserve container, around and under the canopy with fingers and thumb pointing down.
7. Get a good grip on the canopy and stretch it out to arm length. (This frees a couple of stows of the suspension lines.)
8. Lift the canopy up to the side of your head and throw it vigorously *down, out, and in the direction of the spin.* (Many partial malfunctions, particularly of advanced canopies such as the Para-Commander, will cause the main parachute to turn, sometimes quite rapidly and violently.)
9. Reach into the pack and feed out the rest of the lines. A "pumping" action may help the canopy inflate.
10. Once the reserve canopy is fully inflated, you may choose to release the main parachute risers to jettison the main canopy. You can safely land under *both* canopies, but if there are oscillations because of interference between the two canopies, your landing will probably be harder.

As a student, you will have little choice between the two procedures. You will use the procedure you are trained for, but I strongly recommend the breakaway *with the Stevens Cutaway System* as a backup.

I am so strongly biased in favor of the Stevens Cutaway System for students that I urge the beginning student to train *only* at a club or commercial center that requires this system for its students, but USPA doctrine does not go that far. Both systems are safe, with proper training and correct procedures. But I believe the breakaway gives an additional margin of safety that could be vital, especially for students (provided the breakaway is used with the Stevens Cutaway System).

Two points about the procedures for dealing with partial malfunctions cannot be stressed too strongly:

- A *streamer* hardly reduces your rate of descent at all, and there is nothing you can do to clear it. So *don't waste valuable time.* Go immediately to your emergency procedures.
- Many jumpers still use ripcord cable stops. These are devices such as lead sinkers or several turns of rubber stow band. It is attached to the main ripcord cable to keep it from coming all the way out of the cable housing after the pull. It is a very dangerous way of avoiding the loss of a fairly expensive ripcord, because the handle and a length of cable are exposed, just dangling in front of you. Several fatalities have resulted from entanglement of the reserve parachute with this handle and cable.

TOTAL MALFUNCTIONS

A total malfunction is one in which nothing comes out of the parachute container. In the case of a total malfunction, *pull the reserve ripcord immediately.* Do not waste time going through a breakaway procedure (which releases the main canopy) because there is nothing to break away from.

STUDENT TRAINING IN EMERGENCY PROCEDURES

A substantial portion of the student's training time during a first-jump course is devoted to emergency procedures. A suspended harness is absolutely essential for this training. This harness has risers that are attached to the student's harness and approximates the situation of hanging under a parachute.

If you go to a club or commercial center for your first-jump training and find that the suspended harness is not used, go elsewhere. This problem is unusual, however, because people in charge of training who would attempt training without the suspended harness are rare.

Student training in dealing with the total malfunction is actually part of the "six count" drill, which is intended to insure a stable exit from the airplane and a proper dummy ripcord pull on static-line jumps. After the count, "One thousand, two thousand, etc.," the student goes to emergency procedures after six seconds.

The procedure starts with the student bending at the waist, his hand on his reserve ripcord handle, and looking over each shoulder to see if something is coming out of the main parachute container. If not, he pulls the reserve.

Usually the student does not reach the count of six before he feels the opening shock of his parachute. If he does get that far, the chances are very good that he has a *pilot chute hesitation*. When the parachutist falls in a stable, face-to-earth position, a partial vacuum is created over his back. The pilot chute has a spring that causes it to be ejected from the pack, but this partial vacuum might keep it from catching air.

Bending at the waist causes a change in the flow of air over the jumper's back, the pilot chute catches air, and the parachute begins to open immediately. If it does not, of course, a true total malfunction exists, and the parachutist pulls the reserve ripcord.

AUTOMATIC OPENERS

Many clubs and some centers require students, at least on their first several jumps, to be equipped with automatic openers. An automatic opener is a device, usually mounted on the reserve parachute but sometimes used with the main, that is calibrated to activate at about 1,000 to 1,400 feet above the ground. If a parachute has not opened by the time the student gets that low, the device automatically opens a parachute.

Student practices emergency procedures in suspended harness at Stevens School of Sport Parachuting, Oakland, California. (Photo by Eric Anderson)

It is strongly recommended that the automatic opener be used with the *reserve* parachute. If there is some mechanical reason for a total malfunction of the main parachute, the automatic opener is useless. Since the reserve must be inspected and repacked at regular intervals by an FAA-certificated rigger, there is almost never a mechanical reason for failure of the reserve.

If you are a student, I cannot emphasize too strongly that you should refuse to jump at a drop zone where automatic openers are not used. It is your extra margin of safety, and it is my personal opinion that all students should be equipped with automatic openers, at least through their early freefall jumps. While the USPA does not yet require the automatic opener through its Basic Safety Regulations, it does recommend its use. There are specific safety procedures to be followed with the use of the older types of automatic opener, such as the Sentinel. Your Jumpmaster will thoroughly brief you on the use of your opener. These devices are described in detail in Chapter 15.

OTHER SAFETY PROCEDURES

The parachutist must avoid power lines at all costs. He *might* escape electrocution, but his chances are very slim. Much has been written in other books and military manuals about the correct method of setting yourself up for landing on power lines. The only trouble is, they just don't work, so most instructors just tell the student to avoid them and leave it at that. The student is trained in canopy control (steering his parachute), so there is no excuse for landing on power lines.

Since the student is taught to face into the wind, to reduce his speed over the ground during landing, an error in judgment sometimes causes the student to land on power lines, in a tree, or on some other obstacle.

The way to avoid such an error in judgment is this: If there is *any doubt in your mind* that you are going to clear the obstacle, run with the wind until you are *past* it and then turn back into the wind. But the decision must be made at an altitude high enough to allow you to clear the obstacle. Low-altitude decisions can be very dangerous.

There are other safety procedures associated with night jumps, water jumps (including unintentional water landings), and relative work. These procedures are discussed in the chapters dealing with those subjects.

5

First Aid

Emergency procedures such as those discussed in Chapter 4 are designed to keep you alive. Sport parachuting, however, like skiing and other sports, has its injuries, and every parachutist should know at least the fundamentals of first aid on the drop zone.

Dr. W. Scott Piper, III, is the author of a series of articles on parachuting injuries published in *Parachutist*, the official publication of the United States Parachute Association. Dr. Piper, an orthopedic surgeon, a lecturer at the University of Miami School of Medicine, and the physician for the local high school football team, made his first jump in 1958 and is still an active sport parachutist. He has served as team physician for the Cadet Parachute Team of the United States Military Academy at West Point and is now a member of the Everglades Sport Parachuting Club.

This series of three articles is reprinted by permission of Dr. Piper and the United States Parachute Association.

They are meant to be instructive, not alarming.

ANKLE INJURIES[3]

It has been my experience that next to abrasions and contusions (scrapes and lumps), the injured ankle is the most common injury encountered at the DZ.

For simplicity we will consider ankle injuries under two separate categories: sprains and fractures. A *sprain* is an injury to a ligament, and a *fracture* is a broken bone.

There are minor sprains and major sprains, just as there are minor fractures and major fractures. However, never say it is *just* a sprain. *Ligament rupture is just as important as a broken bone.* If the foot is twisted inward on impact, then a sprain is most likely. On the other hand, if the foot is turned outward, the probability of a fracture is greater. Keep in mind that the two are often hard to distinguish and therefore *treat a sprain as if it were a fracture* until the patient can be examined by a physician.

The injury sustained is almost always worse than the jumper feels it is immediately after impact. Consequently, it is quite common for a jumper to belittle a severe sprain or even a fracture and walk off the DZ under his own steam. Later, however, pain and swelling increase. Within an hour, the walk becomes a limp; and a few hours later, the patient is unable to walk at all.

This delayed reaction will also fool anyone attempting to evaluate the ankle immediately after injury. Swelling into the soft tissues after an injury, as well as bleeding from tissue or bone rupture, requires time. In addition, immediately after injury the nerves supplying the ankle as well as the soft tissue and ligaments are in a period of immediate "shock"; therefore, the jumper notices surprisingly little pain. Those attempting to give first aid are likewise fooled and (upon removing the jump boot) they observe an ankle with no swelling or deformity and with minimal pain. This effect can be so pronounced that often trained physicians can arrive at the scene

---

3. Reprinted from *Parachutist*, November 1973.

of the accident too early and miss a diagnosis that a few hours later becomes all too apparent.

The ligament on the outside and front part of the ankle is by far the most commonly injured ligament. This is usually a minor isolated injury which requires little in the way of treatment. There is localized pain and swelling over the dorsal lateral (top and outside) aspect of the ankle. This usually completely subsides by eight days. With such a minor sprain there are no permanent complications. As previously stated, a minor sprain is usually difficult to distinguish from a more serious problem shortly after injury, and it is my strong recommendation that all ankle injuries be examined by a physician and x-rayed.

The jumper with minor ankle sprains should refrain from further jumping activities until all pain and swelling are gone. The reason is simple. A minor sprain represents a partial rupture of a ligament and it is therefore weak. With repeated injury the partial rupture may become complete. Months of treatment might be required, and permanent disability might result. The more moderate sprains are often casted, and these usually require three weeks for healing. Again, the jumper should not return to skydiving until all pain and swelling are gone. Severe ankle sprains imply complete disruption of one or more ligaments, and at a minimum they require eight weeks in the cast. Injuries about the inside of the ankle are usually more severe than those about the outside. Complete rupture of the deltoid ligament sometimes requires surgery. With a moderate or a severe sprain, the ligament may not heal as tight as it was prior to injury. Therefore, with repeated sprains the ankle becomes loose or weak and is subject to repeated injuries with much less stress.

With respect to fractures, most can be treated simply in a short leg walking cast for six to eight weeks. The jumper should allow at least one month after the cast has been removed, allowing the fracture to completely consolidate, before he returns to his jumping activities. Fractures about the inside of the ankle joint frequently lead to bony instability or even complete dislocation of the ankle joint. These injuries usually require surgery, with at least eight weeks in a cast, and jumping should be prohibited for three months after the cast is removed.

Although most minor ankle injuries are undertreated at the DZ, the more severe injury is usually apparent by its very nature. First aid treatment in these cases is most important. *Splint the ankle as it lies; do not attempt to straighten it.* There is great danger that any attempt to straighten the joint will interfere with and impair nerve function and blood supply. The rule about "splinting them where they lie" is particularly valid for compound fractures. In a compound fracture, bone is exposed. There is great temptation to straighten this by applying traction to the foot; however, this allows dirt, clothing and other debris to be dragged into the wound, adding greatly to the medical problem. After the ankle is splinted, it should be elevated as high as is practical. Ice, if available, should be applied outside the splint.

With ankle sprain, ice should be utilized constantly for the first 48 hours. The ice acts by constricting the small blood passages and thereby diminishes the bleeding significantly. The less the initial bleeding and swelling, the more rapid the recovery will be. After 48 hours, the bleeding will no longer be a problem, and the body will be in the healing phase. At this time heat will open up these small blood passages and allow greater circulation in the ankle. This will promote healing, and the recovery will likewise be more rapid.

In summation, ligament rupture is just as important as a broken bone and often leads to more permanent and prolonged disability. An injury should always be treated as if it were a fracture until it can be examined by a physician. Do not jump on minor sprains until all pain and swelling is gone. Splint all dislocations, sprains, and fractures, especially compound fractures, where they lie. Finally and most important, ankle injuries are almost always worse than you think.

HEAD INJURIES[4]

A PLF, done properly, should distribute the forces of impact over five body points, and thus dissipate the energy. However, the key word is *"properly."*

Jumpers manage to bash their heads against various objects in the most exotic ways. The most common head trauma occurs at the DZ when a jumper lands backing up in high winds. He lands on his feet, and for a fraction of a second he is deluded into thinking he has a standup landing. Then the full canopy jerks him over backward and he hits the ground in a manner substantially different from a PLF.

Head injuries are *all potentially life threatening, whether followed by unconsciousness or not.* In addition, head trauma can be very deceptive, as *the damage to the brain and the symptoms are often delayed.* The skull is an unyielding container, and the brain is composed of very delicate tissue. A ruptured blood vessel between the skull and the brain will cause a blood clot that may grow very slowly and eventually apply pressure to the brain. Hence, a jumper may appear well and normal shortly after a head injury; and signs of brain damage may not become apparent until hours, or even days, later.

If the jumper is unconscious for even a very short time following the accident, he has, by definition, a concussion. A concussion is a bruising of the brain and usually is not serious. But *usually* is not good enough. Because there is a chance of forming a blood clot between the brain and the skull, the jumper with a concussion should be grounded for 24 to 48 hours for observation.

If the jumper regains consciousness and then lapses back into an unconscious state, or if he is not unconscious at first but then gradually loses consciousness, then a serious medical emergency exists. *This jumper must be taken to the hospital immediately.*

---

4. Reprinted from *Parachutist*, December 1973.

When checking for possible brain injury, look carefully at both eyes. The pupils are normally equal in size and become smaller when exposed to bright light. Conversely, they dilate in darkness. Hence, normal eyes have pupils which are equal in size and react to changes in light. If one pupil is larger than the other and if it does not constrict with light as much as the other, then increased pressure within the skull is likely. This is obviously a sign of significant head injury, and even though the jumper is conscious and alert at the time, he should be taken immediately to the hospital.

Another danger sign is bleeding or leaking of clear fluid from the nose or the ear. This usually indicates a fracture at the base of the skull and will require treatment by a physician. Nausea or vomiting after a head injury may mean increased pressure within the skull and is likewise an emergency.

In giving first aid to a jumper who is unconscious, one must strongly suspect a broken neck; therefore, treat such a person accordingly. Most important, *do not move the neck of such a person.* The neck should be splinted, and when transporting a patient with a head injury, it is ideal to have the head of the stretcher slightly elevated.

With shock and a head injury, do not elevate the feet. With head injuries as with any serious injury, the jumper should have nothing to eat or drink. This includes even sips of water.

At some DZ's it seems to be stylish for the more experienced jumpers (or those who would like to appear more experienced) to wear a cloth or leather skull cap instead of a helmet. I strongly feel that this practice should be prohibited for obvious reasons. I am reminded of my own experience. When buying my gear, I asked the salesman for an inexpensive helmet. He replied, "What 'sa matter, you got a cheap head?"

BUTT STRIKES[5]

"Butt strike" needs little definition as the colorful term is vir-

---

5. Reprinted from *Parachutist*, March 1974.

tually self-explanatory. As any experienced parachutist knows, a butt strike usually occurs during accuracy jumps when the jumper extends his leg for the disc and inadvertently plants his *gluteus maximus* in the peas [pea gravel used to define the target area]. If this part of the anatomy is the first part of the jumper to strike the ground, then we have a true butt strike. It should be remembered, however, that butt strikes do occur "in other situations." My wife, for example, lifted her legs while trying to cross a paved runway and succeeded in fracturing her *coccyx* (tail bone) when she landed bottom first.

Butt strikes are no laughing matter, as any experienced jumper will tell you. In a normal landing, absorbing the energy of impact is nicely handled by the legs. The feet, the ankles, the knees, and the hips all bend in a springlike fashion, and the energy is absorbed by the surrounding supporting muscles. However, when these energy-absorbing "springs" are eliminated, the jolt to the body is enormous.

For example: Have you ever been walking along reading a book or looking at the sky when you accidentally stepped off a curb or into a small hole? The sudden fall of only a few inches on a fully extended hip and knee is literally enough to rattle your brain. The same mechanism of course applies in a true butt strike, when the legs fail to serve as energy-absorbing devices and all the energy of impact is transferred immediately to the pelvis or the base of the spine.

The bony spinal column is a relatively rigid structure with little ability to absorb energy when it is stressed in its vertical plane. The skull sits on top of the bony spinal column and thus the energy is directly transmitted to it. Skull fractures therefore, while uncommon, are quite possible with a butt strike. The bleeding or leaking of clear fluid from the nose or ear is a strong indication of fracture at the base of the skull.

Ankle injuries are almost always worse than the jumper feels immediately after impact, but just the opposite is true with butt strikes. After a true butt strike, the jumper usually feels one or more of the following:

1. He has broken his pelvis.
2. He has broken his back.
3. He is paralyzed.
4. He is dying.

Fortunately, injury in butt strikes is usually much less severe than the jumper at first thinks. Most of the time the supine figure in the peas merely has the wind knocked out of him, and after a few minutes he recovers and is embarrassed for the delay of the contest.

Conversely, *any or all* of the conditions the jumper initially suspects may actually exist. With a butt strike it is quite possible to break one's hips, pelvis, back, become paralyzed, sustain internal injuries, break one's neck or skull, and even injure the brain. In short, very major injury, though not the usual result of a butt strike, *is a very real possibility*.

Immediately after the patient has made his disastrous landing, he is usually temporarily stunned or dazed. The extent of the injury is not known to either the jumper or to the surrounding onlookers. *All precautions must be taken at this time.* The canopy should be released at the Capewells; do not attempt to remove the jumper from the harness.

It should be obvious that the patient should not be moved at all until the extent of the injury can be ascertained. Should he have broken his back or neck, then moving the patient may result in permanent paralysis that otherwise could be avoided by proper handling. Leave the jumper flat on his back and do not move him.

If he is initially unconscious, then he must be seen by a physician whether or not he subsequently regains consciousness. Any jumper who complains of persistent back, neck, or leg pain should likewise be taken immediately to a physician for appropriate x-rays and diagnosis. It is interesting that the complaint of immediate numbness in both legs is a very common one, and if this clears in a matter of minutes, then the jumper need not seek medical attention, assuming he has no other complaints.

Spinal Injuries

It should be obvious that breaks or dislocations of the bony spinal column are of great significance because they are often associated with damage to the spinal cord. This may lead to paralysis or death. The spinal cord is protected by the spinal column, and as long as the spinal column remains intact, the spinal cord is safe. As the exact diagnosis may be difficult, it would be wise to *treat all suspected spinal injuries as if they were fractures or dislocations.*

There are several signs of spinal injuries:

1. *Pain.* Usually a jumper will complain of pain in the area of the spinal fracture. Occasionally, however, the jumper will be sufficiently stunned from the impact that the pain is not noticeable, and he will not complain of it. This is particularly true if he is lying very still in a position of relative comfort. In this situation the next two signs will be useful. ·

2. *Tenderness.* Gently feel the area of suspected injury. If this causes the jumper increased pain, there is reason to suspect spinal injury, and he should be handled as if his back were broken.

3. *Painful movement.* Most important. *Never try to test painful movement by moving the patient's injured area for him.* As previously stated, moving a broken back may cause pressure on the cord with resulting paralysis. However, if the *patient* makes an attempt to move the injured area and notes increasing pain, then one should strongly suspect a fracture. The patient should not be encouraged to move if he has pain, and he should be splinted immediately for transportation to the hospital.

4. *Deformity.* This is an unusual sign; therefore, the *absence* of deformity in no way rules out the possibility of fracture. Since deformity only occurs with very severe injuries, you might keep in mind that if it looks broken it usually is.

Classic butt strike during competition. (USPA Photo)

5. *Lacerations and contusions (cuts and bruises)*. These are indications of the severity of the force applied to that particular area of the patient's body. Again, like deformity, the absence of cuts and bruises does not rule out the possibility of spinal fracture.
6. *Paralysis*. Again, remember that spinal cord shock from impact is very common and a transitory loss of sensation in the legs is not worrisome. The key word here of course is *transitory* (of brief duration). The jumper should be completely normal within two to three minutes. Any loss of sensation or weakness of muscle power that persists longer than two or three minutes is very ominous. Extreme care must be taken in handling this type of patient.

Care of suspected spinal injuries is similar to that of other major injuries.

First, be sure that the jumper is breathing satisfactorily. If the jumper is having difficulty breathing, and he is found with his head lying in a twisted position, then apply gentle traction to the head while correcting the deformity. If this is insufficient, then lift the chin and slide the jaw forward. Check the jumper's mouth to make sure that there are no obstructions such as loose dentures or a mouth full of peas. (About the only time you should move a patient with a suspected spinal injury is when you need to obtain an airway to allow him to breathe.)

Second, control any serious bleeding by local pressure dressings.

Third, and most important, splint the patient before moving him. Carefully splint the injured spine, avoiding abnormal or excessive motion. Be sure that the injured person is properly splinted and transported on a long backboard or special stretcher without bending or twisting the spine in any direction. It is best to *splint the deformed neck or back in the position of deformity*. Do not try to straighten a deformity simply to make splinting easier or more convenient. Straighten only to help open the airway.

Summary

Most jumpers with a true butt strike initially feel that they have sustained serious injury. However, in reality the vast majority have only a combination of spinal cord shock and the wind knocked out of them, both of which are transient and pass very shortly. However, because of the large amount of energy delivered to the base of the spine, very serious injuries are quite possible. These injuries include fracture or dislocation of the spine, with or without paralysis, and/or head injuries consisting of concussion with or without skull fracture.

Land feet first; it's good for your health.

Aerial view of Pope Valley Parachute Ranch near St. Helena, California. (Photo by Ray Cottingham)

6

Where You Go to Jump

The *1974–75 USPA Directory* lists drop zones in most of the 50 states—178 in all—and 11 in Canada. (The number listed for Canada is probably greatly in error, because 81 Canadian clubs are affiliated with the Canadian Sport Parachuting Association.)

The total number of drop zones is considerably higher in both the United States and Canada, because a number of clubs and centers fail to respond to the survey by the publication deadline of the *Directory*. In addition, since parachuting is a rapidly growing sport, many drop zones come into existence during the two-year period covered by the *Directory*. Of course, some drop zones cease operations during the same period.

There are two general types of parachuting operations: clubs and commerical centers. In the early years of sport parachuting, most drop zone operations were run by clubs. The current trend is toward more commercial centers and fewer clubs.

The only real reason for the existence of a club is to provide the facilities for its members to jump—to find (and pay for) the aircraft support without which there is no parachuting, and to maintain a drop zone. Since clubs are nonprofit organizations, they charge their members jump rates and assess dues only to keep their operations financially solvent.

In addition to the aircraft (usually not owned by the club but arranged for as a business proposition) and the drop zone itself (often rented from the landowner), the club must provide other facilities for its members, such as a parachute packing area, a target (usually pea gravel), a windsock, and equipment storage facilities. Since clubs must keep people coming into the sport to keep their operation alive, they must train students. This means adequate training facilities and an inventory of parachuting equipment for students.

Many drop zones are located on or near airports. These airports are often privately owned, and the airport management sometimes provides land for the drop zone and supplies the jump aircraft. Thus, in such cases the club and the airport have a mutually beneficial arrangement.

While there have been some incidents in which an adjacent landowner has confiscated at gunpoint the parachute gear of the jumper who accidentally landed on his property, a great many landowners go to the opposite extreme and allow the use of their land at little or no cost to the club.

The commercial center has the same problems as the club, but the growth of parachuting has made the center feasible as a business venture. Since the center must pay for a staff and facilities and still make a profit, the costs are likely to be somewhat higher for the jumper. To make the business profitable, there must be a fairly good rate of parachuting activity.

The most lucrative part of the business of many centers is in training students, since the margin of profit in this area is higher than that derived from equipment sales and rental and the provision of aircraft support for experienced jumpers. While the jump rates for experienced jumpers may be no higher than those charged by clubs, the beginning parachutist's student career is likely to be a lot more expensive than that of a student associated with a club.

Many commercial centers are fairly small operations, often open only on weekends and holidays; others are open every day or are closed only on one day during the week.

Under current rules of the United States Parachute Association, clubs (but not centers) may be USPA-affiliated. To be eligible for affiliation, the club must have at least 10 members, 75 percent of the membership must be USPA members, and the club must agree to comply with all rules and regulations of the national organization. Benefits of affiliation include priority in bidding for Conference and National Championships, conventions, meetings, or other USPA activities, and discounts on the purchase or rental of films and other materials provided by the national organization.

While many nonaffiliated clubs are as safe as those with USPA affiliation (and some affiliated clubs fall short of their responsibilities), the beginning parachutist has more assurance that adequate standards of safety are maintained if he jumps with an affiliated club. With the growth of commercial centers, USPA is quite likely to extend affiliation to centers as well as clubs.

The *1974–75 USPA Directory* lists all centers and all clubs, whether affiliated or not, about which information is available. The following list of drop zones includes most centers and clubs in the United States and a substantial number in Canada. The list gives only the name and location of each drop zone and identifies it as a club or commercial center.

For full information about drop zones in the United States, including facilities available, type of aircraft, mail address, and other details, order the *1974–75 USPA Directory*, which costs $2.00, from the United States Parachute Association, P.O. Box 109, Monterey, California 93940. The *Directory* also lists Area Safety Officers, Instructor/Examiners, USPA-affiliated clubs, FAA offices, and national aero-clubs and parachuting organizations in other countries.

For further information about Canadian drop zones, write to the Canadian Sport Parachuting Association, P.O. Box 848, Burlington, Ontario, Canada.

UNITED STATES

Alabama

Birmingham, Sylacauga Municipal Airport. Club.
Cairns Army Airfield, Ft. Rucker. Military club.
Eutaw Airport, Eutaw. Club.
Grandview Sport Parachute Center, Elberta. Club.
Headland Drop Zone, Headland Airport. Commercial.

Alaska

Jack O'Brian's Field, Fairbanks. Club.

Arizona

Arizona Para-Center, Coolidge-Florence Municipal Airport.
    Commercial.
Columbine Para Center, Casa Grande Municipal Airport.
    Commercial.
Rim Rock DZ, Rim Rock. Club.
Sky-Hi Pioneers, Phoenix. Club.
U.S. Parachute Service, Phoenix. Commercial.

Arkansas

Kizer Field, Prescott. Club.

California

Antioch Sport Parachute Center, Antioch Airport. Commercial.
Borderland Air Sports Center, Otay Lakes, San Diego. Commercial.
California Parachute Club, Livermore. Club.
Corning DZ, Corning Municipal Airport. Club.
Elsinore Paracenter, Elsinore. Commercial.
Ft. Ord SPC/Hunter Ligget Para Club, Ft. Ord. Military club.
Lincoln, Lincoln. Commercial.

Perris Valley, Perris Valley. Commercial.
Pope Valley Parachute Ranch, Pope Valley. Commercial.
Santa Nella DZ, Santa Nella. Commercial.
Taft School of Sport Parachuting, Taft. Commercial.
Yolo DZ, Yolo County Airport. Commercial.

Colorado

Air Force Academy, U.S. Air Force Academy. Military club.
Free Flight Sport Aviation, Littleton. Commercial.
Mountain Para Center, Greeley. Commercial.

Connecticut

Connecticut Parachutists, Inc. DZ, Ellington Airport. Club.

Florida

Buchan Airport, Englewood. Club.
Central Florida Para Center, Eustis. Commercial.
Deland Sport Parachute Center, Deland. Commercial.
Palatka Para-Center, Palatka. Commercial.
Palm Beach Sport Parachutists, Delray Beach. Club.
Riverview, Riverview. Club.
South Florida Parachute Center, Indiantown. Commercial.
Zephyrhills Para Center, Zephyrhills Municipal Airport.
   Commercial.

Georgia

Dalton Para Center, Dalton. Commercial.
Fryar DZ, Ft. Benning. Military club.
Greene County Sport Center, Locust Grove. Commercial.
Swamp Hollow, Cairo. Commercial.
Triple "H" DZ, near Locust Grove, south of Atlanta. Commercial.

Hawaii

Hickam AFB Sport Parachute Club
Tropic Lightning Sport Parachute Club

Idaho

Athol Para Center, Henley Aerodrome, 15 miles north of Coeur d'Alene. Commercial.

Illinois

Archway Sport Parachute Center, Sparta. Commercial.
Doc Wronke's Flying Horse Farm, Homer. Commercial.
Greater St. Louis Parachute Club, Greenville Airport. Club.
Hinckley, Hinckley. Commercial.
Illinois Valley Para Center, Pekin. Commercial.
Maple Grove, Isley Airport, 18 miles east of Effingham. Commercial.
Trackers, Inc., Annawan. Commercial.
Warsaw DZ, Warsaw. Club.
Watseka-Kankakee Skydivers, Clifton. Club.

Indiana

Ace Para Center, Anderson. Commercial.
Brown Road Airport, New Castle. Club.
Greencastle Municipal Airport, 30 miles west of Indianapolis. Club.
Para-Sport Para Club, Inc., 20 miles south of Ft. Wayne. Commercial.

Iowa

Central Iowa Skydivers, Perry Municipal Airport, Perry. Club.
Eastern Iowa Para-Hawks, Mathews Memorial Airport, Tipton. Club.
Ekman Field, 8 miles east of Des Moines. Club.
Iowa Parachute Team DZ, Iowa City. Club.

Kansas

Flanagan/Leal DZ, Marshall Army Airfield, Ft. Riley. Military club.
Herington Sky Sports, Herington Municipal Airport, Herington. Commercial.
Wichita Para Center, Harrison Field, Valley Center. Commercial.

Kentucky

Greene County Sport Parachute Center of Kentucky, Bardstown. Commercial.

Louisiana

Delta Skydivers, Raceland. Club.
Southern Parachute Center, Covington. Commercial.

Maine

Millinocket Airport, Millinocket. Commercial.
Pelicanland, Ridgely. Commercial.
Woodbine Sport Parachute Center, Woodbine. Club.

Massachusetts

Orange Para Center, Orange. Commercial.
Taunton Jump Center, Taunton Municipal Airport, Taunton. Club.

Michigan

Austin Lake Skydivers, Kalamazoo. Club.
Elite Skydiving Club, Gregory. Club.
Michigan State University Sport Parachute Club, Charlotte. Club.
Midwest Sport Parachute Center, Gradolph Airport, Petersburg. Commercial.
Otisville-Rixport, Otisville. Commercial.
Parachuting Service, Tecumseh. Commercial.
Parahawks Para Center, Salem Municipal Airport, Salem. Commercial.
West Michigan Sport Parachute Center, Van's Airport, Coopersville. Commercial.

Minnesota

Trout Air Skydivers, Forest Lake. Club.

Mississippi

Circle M Para Club, Madison. Club.

Grenada Lake Sport Parachute Club, Grenada Municipal Airport, Grenada. Club.
Gulf Coast Parachute Association, Jackson County Airport, Pascagoula. Club.

Missouri

Central Missouri Para Center, Fulton. Commercial.
Ka-Mo Sport Parachute Club, Kansas City. Club.
Ripcord West, Washington. Commercial.

Montana

Billings Para Center, Litton Ranch, 15 miles southeast of Billings. Commercial.
Osprey Sport Parachute Club, Kalispell Municipal Airport, Kalispell. Club.

Nebraska

Arrow Airport, Lincoln. Club.
Omaha Sky Divers, South Omaha Airport, Papillion. Club.

Nevada

Las Vegas Sport Parachute Club, Las Vegas. Club.
Nevada Sky Divers, Carson City. Club.

New Jersey

East Coast Para Center, Fairton. Commercial.
Lakehurst, Ft. Monmouth. Military club.
Lakewood Sport Parachute Center, Lakewood. Commercial.
N.A.S., Lakehurst, Lakehurst. Military club.

New Mexico

New Mexico Sport Parachute Center, Moriarty. Club.
Valencia Community Airpark, Valencia. Club.
West Mesa, Albuquerque. Club.

New York

Albany Skydiving Center, Sloansville. Commercial.
Fred McKlintok Skydiving, Gardiner. Commercial.
Galeville DZ, Wallkill. Military club.
Hamlin DZ, Hamlin. Club.
Hudson Valley Skydivers, Sha-Wan-Ga Valley Airport,
   Bloomingburg. Club.
L.A.G.N.A.F. Skydivers, Ava Airport, Ava. Club.
Malone Para Center, Malone. Commercial.
Oneida Lake Water DZ, Oneida Lake. Club.
Seneca Sport Parachute Club, Seneca Falls Airport, Seneca Falls.
   Commercial.
Southern Tier Skydivers, Ceres Airport, Olean. Commercial.
Stormville Para Center, Stormville. Commercial.

North Carolina

Charlotte Skydivers, Inc., Midland. Commercial.
Franklin County Sport Parachute Center, Louisburg. Commercial.
Laurinburg-Maxton Airport, Laurinburg. Commercial.
Raeford Drop Zone, Raeford. Club.
Roanoke Rapids Para-Center, Halifax County Airport, Roanoke
   Rapids. Commercial.
St. Mere Eglise DZ, Ft. Bragg. Military club.
Tar Heel Sport Parachute Center, Trinity. Commercial.

North Dakota

Fort Pembina Airport, Pembina. Commercial.
Valley Skydivers, Inc., Kindred. Club.

Ohio

Alliance Sport Parachute Club, Salem. Club.
Auglaize County Sport Parachute Center, Neil Armstrong Airport,
   New Knoxville. Club.
Carol's DZ, Mansfield Airport, Mansfield. Club.
Cleveland Sport Parachute Center, Parkman. Commercial.
Greene Country Sport Parachute Center, Gallopolis. Commercial.
Greene Country Sport Parachute Center, Xenia. Commercial.

Oklahoma

Ellis-Guthrie DZ, Guthrie. Club.
Ft. Sill Sport Parachute Club, Ft. Sill. Military club.
Lee's Grandma's, Guthrie. Club.

Oregon

Ashland Municipal Airport, Ashland. Club.
Beagle Sky Ranch, Medford. Commercial.
Emerald Sky Divers, Daniels Field, Springfield. Club.
Pacific Parachute Center, Sheridan. Commercial.
Western Sport Parachute Center, Molalla. Commercial.

Pennsylvania

Kiski Sport Parachute Center, Vandergrift. Club.
Laurel Highlands Skydivers, Somerset. Club.
Lewisburg DZ, Lewisburg. Club.
Maytown Sport Parachute Club, Maytown. Club.
New Hanover Airport, New Hanover. Club.
Northeast Pennsylvania Ripcords, Hazleton. Club.
Penn's Cave/Penn State, Centre Hall. Club.
York Para Center, Thomasville. Commercial.

South Carolina

Central Carolina Sport Parachute Club, Lugoff. Club.
Oconee-Clemson Airport, Clemson. Club.

South Dakota

South Dakota Skydivers, Inc., Marv Skiie Airport, Lennox. Club.

Tennessee

Decker Farm Airport, Jonesboro. Commercial.
Humboldt DZ, Humboldt. Commercial.
Knoxville Parachute Club, Knoxville. Club.
Tri-State Para Center, Covington. Commercial.

Texas

Alamo Skydivers, Inc., Pleasanton Municipal Airport, Pleasanton. Commercial.
Austin Para Center, Bird's Nest Airport, Austin. Commercial.
Bear Creek Skydivers, Weiser Airpark, Houston. Club.
Cedar Hill DZ, Cedar Hill. Club.
Elmdale Paracenter and Service, Abilene. Commercial.
Fort Hood Sport Parachute Club, W. Ft. Hood. Military club.
McCombs DZ, El Paso. Club.
Para Center of the Southwest, Inc., Cleveland Municipal Airport, Cleveland. Commercial.
Skyhawks Parachute Club, Beaumont Municipal Airport, Beaumont. Club.

Utah

Alta Skydiving Center, Salt Lake City. Commercial.

Virginia

Marine Corps Development Center DZ, Quantico. Military club.
New River Valley Para Center, Dublin. Commercial.
Norfolk Sport Parachute Club, Suffolk Municipal Airport, Suffolk. Club.
St. Michael's Angels Sport Parachute Club, Flying Circus Aerodrome, Fredericksburg. Club.
Shenandoah Valley Para Center, Waynesboro Airport, Waynesboro. Club.

Virgin Islands

Morningstar Beach, St. Thomas. Club.

Washington

Connell Sky Divers, Connell. Club.
Eggers Field, Pullman. Club.
Herbie's Para Center, Richland Airport, Richland. Club.
Seattle Sky Divers, Snohomish. Club.
Snohomish Para Center, Snohomish. Club.

Wisconsin

Apollo DZ, Superior. Club.
Big Patch Parachute Club, Platteville. Club.
East Troy Municipal Airport, East Troy. Club.
Indianhead Skydivers, Wissota Airport, Chippewa Falls. Club.
Math-Aire Field, northeast of Madison. Club.
Parachuting, Inc., Rainbow Airport, south of Milwaukee.
    Commercial.
Para-Naut DZ, Oshkosh. Commercial.
Southern Wisconsin Skyhawks, Inc., Winfield Airport, Bristol.
    Commercial.
Waunakee Airport, Waunakee. Club.

Wyoming

Casper Sport Parachute Club, Harford Field, Casper. Club.
Hole in the Sky Gang DZ, Howe Field, Laramie. Club.

CANADA

Alberta

Black Bear Sport Parachute Club, Calgary. Club.
Calgary Parachute Club, Calgary. Club.
C.F.B. Cold Lake Parachute Club, Medley. Club.
C.F.B. Edmonton Sport Parachute Club, Lancaster Park. Club.
Edmonton Parachute Club, Edmonton. Club.
Skyline Sport Parachute Club, Claresholm. Club.

British Columbia

Abbotsford Sport Parachute Centre, Abbotsford. Commercial.
British Columbia School of Sport Parachuting, Vancouver.
    Commercial.
Chilliwack Skydivers, Chilliwack. Club.
Comox Parachute Centre, Comox. Club.
Kamloops Sport Parachute Club, Kamloops. Club.
Prince George Skydiving Club, Prince George. Club.
University of British Columbia Sport Parachute Club, Vancouver.
    Club.

Victoria Skydiving Club, Victoria. Club.

Manitoba

Brandon Sport Parachute Club, Brandon. Club.
Morris Skydivers, Winnipeg. Club.
Parachute Manitoba, Winnipeg. Club.

New Brunswick

C.T.C. Military Parachute Club, Oromocto. Club.
University of New Brunswick Sport Parachute Club, Fredericton.
   Club.

Nova Scotia

Kingfisher Sport Parachute Club, Halifax. Club.
Seagull Skydiving Club, Sydney. Club.
Shearwater Sport Parachute Club, Shearwater. Club.

Ontario

Bruce County Skydivers, Kincardine. Club.
Burnaby School of Sport Parachuting, Mississauga. Club.
Cambrian College Parachute Club, Sudbury. Club.
Carleton University Sport Parachute Club, Ottawa. Club.
C.F.B. North Bay Sport Parachute Club, Hornell Heights. Club.
Gananoque Sport Parachuting Centre, Gananoque. Commercial.
Grand Valley Sport Parachute Club, Simcoe. Club.
Hamilton Sport Parachute Club, Inc., Hamilton. Club.
Huronia Sport Parachute Club, Midland. Club.
Nipissing Skydivers, Hornell Heights. Club.
Ottawa Sport Parachutists, Ottawa. Club.
Parachute Association of Toronto, Toronto. Club.
Paralgonquin, Ottawa. Club.
Phoenix Parachute Club, Toronto. Club.
Queens University Skydiving Club, Kingston. Club.
St. Catharines Parachute Club, St. Catharines. Club.
University of Western Ontario Sport Parachute Club, London.
   Club.

Prince Edward Island

C.F.B. Summerside Sport Parachute Club, Slemon Park. Club.

Quebec

Concordia Skydivers, Montreal. Club.
Les Cerfs Volants, Cte. Levis. Club.
Les Hommes Volants, Montreal. Club.
McGill Skydiving Club, Montreal. Club.
St. Marie Skydivers, Longueuil. Club.

Saskatchewan

Country Aero Sport Parachute Club, Regina Beach. Club.
Saskatoon Skydivers, Saskatoon. Club.
Swift Current Skydiving Club, Swift Current. Club.

7

Competition

Competition is very much a part of the sport parachuting scene. Although the pure fun of jumping is enough for some parachutists, most eventually get into competition, at least on the local level. (There are even competitions for students.)

Competition is divided into three categories: accuracy, style, and relative work.

ACCURACY

Accuracy competition goes back to the early days of sport parachuting and has long been the most popular area of competition, although interest in relative work competition is rapidly increasing. The accuracy competitor tries to steer his parachute to score a "dead center," which means he hits a disc measuring 10 centimeters (3.94 inches) in diameter.

The competitor's strike is measured in meters, to the nearest centimeter, and the jumper's *first* point of contact with the

Competitor Jimmy Davis heads for the disc. (Photo by Ray Cottingham)

ground is the measured strike. (If one foot hits the disc, and the other foot hits *first*, 10 centimeters away, his score is 0.10, not 0.00.)

Normally a competitor's strike is not measured beyond 10 meters from the disc. In fact, most competitions are won by *centimeters*. During the Eleventh World Parachuting Championships in 1972, R. V. Kumba of Czechoslovakia scored *nine* dead centers in a row, then blew it on the tenth jump with a 1.72-meter hit, sliding into tenth place.

In the 1973 U.S. Nationals, John Wolfe scored nine dead centers (not consecutive) and one hit of 0.06 for a 10-round total of 6 centimeters. In the same competition, Leon Riche finished second with a total of 16 centimeters, and Clarence M. Solis had a third-place total of 35 centimeters.

Facing page. Sherman Hawkins is awarded a dead center disc at the 1970 U.S. Nationals. (Photo by Chip Maury)

Judges prepare to mark an accuracy jump of a competitor flying the Para-Plane Cloud. (Photo by Andy Keech)

Student accuracy competition usually involves another system of measurement called "hit and run." Each student lands and runs to touch the disc, and the shortest time wins.

The basic techniques of accuracy competition are discussed in Chapter 8.

Clayton Schoelpple, 1972 World Champion, buries a disc. (Photo by Jerry Irwin)

Competitor buries himself in the pea gravel. (Photo by Joe Gonzales)

STYLE

As accuracy demands skill in maneuvering the parachute, style competition measures the skill with which the parachutist controls his body in freefall. Style is judged by the speed and precision with which the competitor completes an "international series" of six maneuvers done in sequence. The series consists of two 360-degree turns in opposite directions, a back loop, two more full turns, and another back loop. A pair

Video recording has become a valuable tool in judging style. (Photo by Ross Yost)

of 360-degree turns in opposite directions is called a "figure eight."

Judging is by means of an optical device called a telemeter, sometimes supplemented by video recording and evaluation. The stylist is timed from start to finish of the series, to the nearest tenth of a second. The base time is then adjusted by assessing penalties for errors in precision, such as being off heading during a maneuver or by under- or overshooting the maneuver.

Depending on the severity of the error, the penalty might be anything from 0.2 second to the maximum measured time of 16 seconds. A 16-second penalty, called a "zap," might be assessed for performing the wrong sequence of maneuvers or for a violation of safety, such as opening too low.

The world's top competitors in style turn in times in the range of 7 or 8 seconds, with a few competitors occasionally turning in the 6s. A 6-second style jump is comparable to the 4-minute mile. Like the 4-minute mile, this lower barrier has been broken; and as techniques are refined, more and more stylists will be able to shorten their times.

The basic techniques of style competition are discussed in Chapter 9.

RELATIVE WORK

Relative work, like style, is a freefall activity. Unlike style, which is an individual event, relative work is performed by two or more jumpers. Local competition in relative work varies greatly. It may be as simple as the baton pass or egg pass or as demanding as 10-man speed stars or 4-man sequential relative work.

A star is actually a circle, since it is composed of a number of parachutists whose hands are joined in freefall. In competition, the star might be composed of any number, with 4-man and 10-man stars most frequently required.

Sequential relative work is usually performed by a team of four jumpers. This event usually requires the team to form a

The diamond is one of the four-man formations in national competition. (Photo by Chip Maury)

star, break off, and perform a second (and different) formation. The more common formations in sequential relative work are the star, the Murphy's star (one jumper facing outward instead of toward the center of the star), the caterpillar (a line in which each jumper grips the thighs of the jumper in front of him), the diamond, and the line.

Sometimes relative work is combined with accuracy. The team is judged by the speed and precision with which it performs the relative work maneuvers, and then the team members are individually judged in accuracy.

The basic techniques of relative work are discussed in Chapter 10.

LEVELS OF COMPETITION

Competition at the local (club) level is almost endlessly variable in the nature of the events. Trophies are usually awarded the top placers, but "money meets," in which cash prizes are awarded, are becoming more popular.

Above the local level, the competition events are more standardized. While a number of large meets are annual affairs, the higher level meets regularly held in the United States each year are the Conference Parachuting Championships, the U.S. National Parachuting Championships, and the National Collegiate Parachuting Championships.

Conference Parachuting Championships

The United States is divided into 12 conferences, each of which chooses its best competitors for the U.S. Nationals. The purpose of the Conference Championships is to decide who shall compete at the nationals.

U.S. National Parachuting Championships

The purpose of the U.S. Nationals is to select the teams that represent the United States in international competition. At the same time, of course, champions in style, accuracy, and relative work are designated.

In both conference and national championships, men and women compete in separate categories, except that the relative work events include both men and women.

National Collegiate Parachuting Championships

Competitors in the Collegiate Nationals must be full-time undergraduate students. The competition is sponsored by the National Collegiate Parachuting League, an affiliate of USPA.

There are two classes of competition in the Collegiate Nationals, intermediate and advanced. The competition includes style, accuracy, and relative work; and there are no separate categories for men and women.

International Competition

The Federation Aeronautique Internationale (FAI) sponsors

World Parachuting Championships (which include style and accuracy) in even-numbered years and World Parachuting Championships of Relative Work in odd-numbered years. A summary of the World Parachuting Championships is provided in Appendix B.

In addition to the World Championships, there are a number of other regular international parachuting competitions. The most notable of these include: the Adriatic Cup, held in odd-numbered years at Portoroz, Yugoslavia; the Pan-American Championships, held in odd-numbered years in the Americas; and the International Military Sports Council (CISM) meet, for military competitors only, held in even-numbered years in various nations having membership in CISM.

UH-1H "Huey" helicopters were used as jump aircraft at the Eleventh World Parachuting Championships at Tahlequah, Oklahoma in 1972. (Photo by Andy Keech)

Judges ponder a
difficult decision.
(Photo by Joe
Gonzales)

JUDGING

Without judges, there would be no competition. Thus a system of establishing judging ratings is essential to sport parachuting.

There are three levels of judges above the local level in the United States: Conference, National, and FAI (International) Judges.

Before a judge can officiate as a Principal Judge at the U.S. nationals, he must go through a training program, held concurrently with the nationals. Each person in the Training Judge Program serves an apprenticeship at the nationals and is evaluated. To win a slot as a Principal Judge at the nationals in a given year, the candidate must have served as a Principal Judge at a previous nationals or receive an acceptable evaluation upon completion of the Training Judge Program.

Judges at the international level are designated by the FAI. The recommendations of member nations are generally accepted, and these recommendations go to those judges regarded as most competent. To be eligible as an FAI Judge, the candidate must be rated as a National Judge.

8

Techniques for Competition Accuracy

by Dick Williams

Accuracy was the first of the competition events, and continues to be favored by many sport parachutists. While most competitors in the individual events at the U.S. National Championships compete in both accuracy and style, it is possible to qualify in accuracy (or style) alone.

The student is introduced to the subject of canopy control—steering the parachute—even before his first jump. As a matter of safety, he must know how to avoid obstacles and find a safe landing location. As a parachutist's education progresses and he becomes more adept in the basic techniques of handling the canopy, such as steering, braking, stalling, and sinking, and graduates to a more maneuverable canopy such as the Para-Commander, he often becomes interested in accuracy competition.

It is very important to get started correctly in the techniques of accuracy. While I have competed in accuracy at levels short

Facing page. Competitor has the dead center "wired." (Photo by Andy Keech)

of the U.S. Nationals, I hardly qualify as an expert. Therefore, I have invited an expert to share his knowledge with you.

Dick Williams is no stranger to the world of accuracy competition. At the time he wrote this guest chapter, he had logged over 235 dead center jumps out of a total of 1,230. He placed second overall (style and accuracy combination) in the National Collegiate Parachuting Championships of both 1964 and 1965 and was a member of the 1965 West Point National Collegiate Sport Parachute Championship Team. He was the California Accuracy Champion of 1972 and has won numerous other meets.

A resident of Monterey, California, Mr. Williams holds the elite rating of USPA Instructor/Examiner. He is an FAA-certificated Master Parachute Rigger and a commercial pilot. He is married to the former Joan Emmack, one of the top women competitors in the United States.

Charles W. Ryan

Style and relative work jumps, which involve freefall maneuvering, require the parachute only as a means of safely completing the descent. Accuracy, on the other hand, depends primarily on the capabilities of the parachute and the skill of the parachutist, who must maneuver his canopy to land close to the disc.

The object of accuracy is not to "get the disc," but to achieve consistency to the point that dead centers are part of the "gravy" to be heaped on top of many short-centimeter jumps. A study of major competitions will reveal that the most consistently accurate performer wins most of the time. Naturally, the dead center is a good indicator of performance. A jumper will often ask a more experienced jumper to watch his approach that results in a dead center, though many basic rules were violated. The usual comment is, "You got the disc; I guess it was okay."

You must be an absolute master of your parachute before you can expect to become consistent. By making a large number of jumps, under varying conditions, in the shortest possible time, you learn how to trim the canopy, when the canopy stalls, how it recovers, and how to achieve a maximum sink without losing control of the canopy. You should also learn to base your jump plan on observed conditions and develop an instinctive "feel" for the correct exit point. Use your observations on wind speed and direction, terrain effects, density altitude effects on lift, prominent landmarks for use in both spotting and setting up a final approach, and the effectiveness of techniques being used by other competitors with similar canopies to set up a practical plan of action.

Wind velocity (speed and direction) is probably the most important factor to consider. If you don't know the wind, you have little chance of an accurate jump. Conditions at parachute meets vary widely—from light and variable winds, with no definite wind direction, to high winds with shears and significant changes in direction from the upper winds to the ground winds. Regardless of the conditions, you can deter-

John Wolfe, 1973 U.S. Accuracy Champion, scores one of his nine dead centers. The single miss was a 6-centimeter mark. (Photo by Warren Doud)

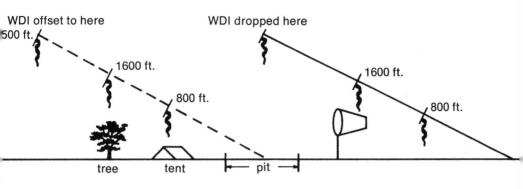

WDI offset to here
500 ft.

WDI dropped here

1600 ft.

1600 ft.

800 ft.

800 ft.

tree   tent |← pit →|

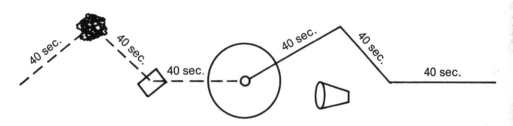

40 sec.   40 sec.   40 sec.   40 sec.   40 sec.

40 sec.   40 sec.

Figure 1. WDI observation

mine an optimal ground track before you ever climb into the aircraft.

When you observe the descent of the wind drift indicator (WDI), you should time it and also note any changes of direction. Then you can plot an opening point on the drop zone photomap and determine a probable approach path. See Figure 1 for an example of this plot. You will notice that the WDI has a constant rate of descent and should be questioned only when the total drop time is more than 2½ minutes or less than 2 minutes. In Figure 1, the wind speeds for each leg are the same, with deviation only in *direction*.

After you plot the winds, you should pick out prominent reference points to guide your travel over the ground during the descent. You should plan to be over specific points on the ground at specific altitudes. This will naturally require that you carry and use an altimeter. Failure to use every advantage available to you is a definite error. Use of an altimeter is mandatory for the serious novice accuracy jumper.

Once you have prepared your plan, you must be aware of several low-altitude effects on the accuracy approach. *Terrain features* such as hills and buildings, which are upwind of the target, might cause turbulence along the approach path, creating some imbalance in your expected smooth approach. The best way to counter turbulence and gusts is to keep right on driving through them, complying with the jump plan. If the target area requires an approach across hard-surface runways, followed by green grass before you come into the peas, be sure to count on lift or sink when you are over these areas. Some pits have a characteristic sinking or lifting effect on the canopy during the short final approach to the target. To pick this up, observe other competitors or make a few practice jumps on the drop zone before the meet.

Thermal conditions affect all wind conditions but are less critical when winds are over 8 miles per hour. Remember that a thermal goes straight up when zero winds exist but leans with the wind as velocity increases. (See Figure 2.) Plan your approach so that you can compensate for the lift or sink of thermals by making the final approach altitude either higher or lower.

Another low-altitude consideration is the *high side of the wind line.* The wind line is defined by the random oscillations of the wind back and forth across a neutral line through the center of the target. (See Figure 3.) This definition is sufficient to get you into the pit, but in most cases you will experience a slide off to the side during the last few seconds of the approach. In most cases, if you are not moving in the saddle or reaching high, the slide is caused by being on the low-speed side of the wind cone.

Under ideal conditions, the wind speed will remain con-

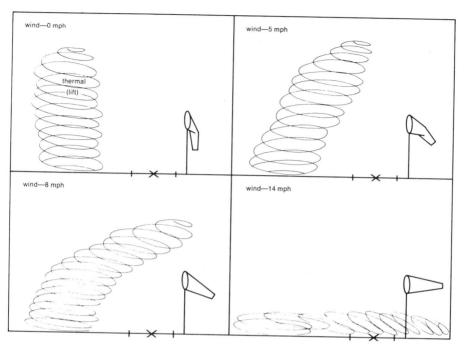

Figure 2. Thermals

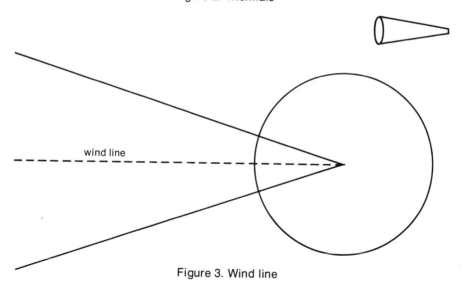

Figure 3. Wind line

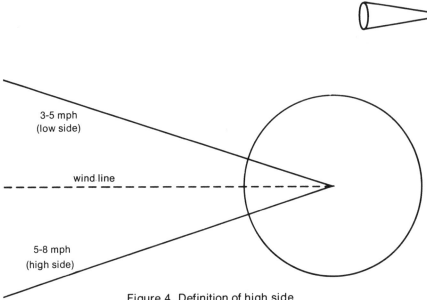

Figure 4. Definition of high side

stant as the direction shifts back and forth across the wind line. This makes it easy for you to stay within the limits of the cone until you are on final approach. But the wind speed is usually *higher* on one side of the cone than on the other. (See Figure 4.) As the wind shifts to the high side and increases in speed, the parachutist who is on the low side will find himself being pushed off to that side and *away from the disc*. (See Figure 5.) To avoid this situation, you must learn to notice subtle changes in your speed over the ground during the final approach so you can move to the high side of the wind line.

Density altitude is a critical factor in planning the final approach. As the density altitude increases, the canopy descends more rapidly. If you know how your canopy performs at a sea-level drop zone and then attempt to use a similar approach at a higher altitude drop zone, you will find yourself falling out short of your intended landing point.

To calculate density altitude you need a density altitude

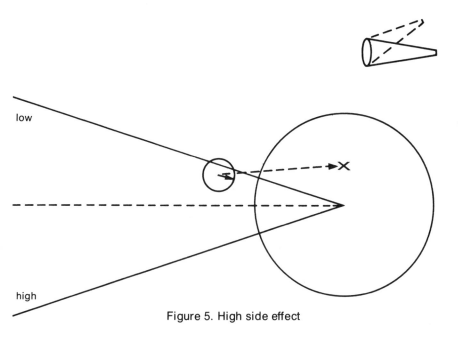

Figure 5. High side effect

chart or calculator, which can be obtained from the pilot shop at most airports. Then, at the drop zone where you are jumping, set an aircraft altimeter to 29.92 in the Kollsman window and read the pressure altitude on the altimeter scale. (The atmospheric pressure with "normal" sea-level conditions is 29.92 inches of mercury.) Enter your density altitude chart with the pressure altitude and the outside air temperature, and you will have density altitude.

For example, assume you are jumping regularly on a drop zone which is 1,500 feet above sea level. When you check the aircraft altimeter to calculate the density altitude, you find that the *pressure altitude* is 2,200 feet above sea level. But the thermometer is hovering around 95° F, and everyone seems to be falling short of the disc. Upon entering the density altitude chart with your figures of 2,200 feet and 95°, you find that the *density altitude* is 4,500 feet above sea level! That is, the *effective* elevation is three times that of your home drop zone.

Dick Williams concentrates on final accuracy approach. (Photo by T. E. Peiffer)

The opposite is true if you usually jump at a high-altitude drop zone and go to a competition on a drop zone which is near sea level. *If you do not consider density altitudes*, you will most likely pass over the disc and land beyond it.

The *stall point* of your canopy (the point at which your canopy loses lift) will vary with the altitude and must be attainable regardless of the density altitude. Therefore, if the canopy is trimmed for a low density altitude, the stall point will be attainable at all higher density altitudes.

Knowledge of local conditions will yield an excellent base of information from which to establish an approach plan. The ideal approach will be made from *half or more brakes* (the halfway point between no pressure and maximum pressure on the steering lines) on the canopy and will follow predetermined check points, with the final approach being either exactly on the wind line or on the high side of the wind cone. During the last few seconds, the approach requires more and more brakes until the stall point is reached a moment before making contact with the ground. (See Figure 6.) You will notice that the approach path *does not remain constant* during the last 100 feet; it is rounded off into a steep drop in on top of

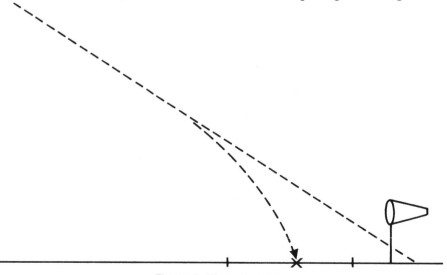

Figure 6. High approach

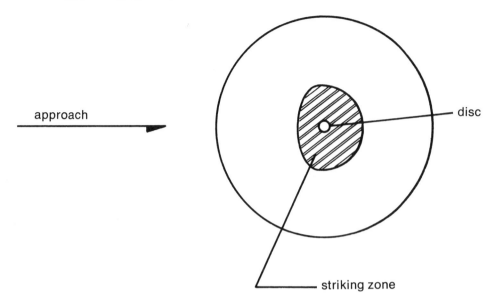

approach

disc

striking zone

Figure 7. Striking zone

the target area. If you continue on a normal flight path, you will overshoot the target and land a few meters past the disc. A maximum sink rate should be achieved at the instant of landing.

One of the biggest problems encountered by a parachutist attempting accuracy is the intense concentration on the yellow disc, which shuts off other valuable bits of information that could have helped avoid an impending problem. The way to resolve this form of *target fixation* (and to relax) is to aim at an *area* called a striking zone. This striking zone is the area around the disc that the parachutist can reach normally without a layout. (The striking zone usually measures about one meter to the front and to the sides and one-half meter to the rear.) If this zone is superimposed over the disc, you see a large area that the jumper is responsible for reaching. Once you have developed the capability to arrive consistently in this striking zone, it will only be a matter of foot placement to get the dead center. (See Figure 7.) The striking zone is placed with the disc as its center because the ideal approach calls for a vertical landing on the disc with no reaching. As wind velocity increases, this goal is more difficult to achieve.

The last point to consider is very important: The jumper who is smooth in all his control movements is usually either an excellent accuracy jumper or the complete opposite. The parachutist who flies himself into the pit smoothly but is not inside the striking zone because of his lack of aggressiveness is missing the entire point of accuracy competition. With possible changes in the wind and the lift of the canopy as you approach the target, you must make canopy control corrections. The closer to the pit, the more violently the corrections must be made. This is especially true because of the lag in control deflection and canopy response. The object is to get inside the striking zone and as close to the disc as possible. This re-

Dick Williams nails another disc at the California Parachute Club's 15th Annual Far Western Competition. (Photo by T. E. Peiffer)

quires a "hank" on the toggles to turn, stop, or slide to the desired landing point. Superimpose an imaginary bubble over the striking zone. You must pierce this bubble and drive not only your foot but your whole body down and through it.

The stand-up landing has no place in accuracy competition unless you can achieve well over 90 percent dead centers. The corrections needed at or below 15 feet above the disc should be exaggerated to ensure an immediate response. A violent turn or stall will not hurt you if it is done from 75 percent brakes or more *and if you are below 15 feet.*

In summary, to become an accomplished accuracy competitor you must:

- observe all conditions in and around the drop zone environment
- develop and comply with a jump plan
- make the approach on the high side of the wind line
- vary the steepness of approach to compensate for density altitude
- aim at the striking zone
- attack the disc
- *enjoy winning*

Good luck!

9

Style

by Debby Schmidt
and James L. Hayhurst

For many years, parachuting competition included only the individual events, style and accuracy. In almost all competitions at levels lower than the U.S. National Championships, there are fewer competitors in style than in accuracy—perhaps because excellence is more difficult to achieve in this event.

As in accuracy, it is very important to learn correct techniques from the beginning. It is extremely difficult to "unlearn" fundamental errors. Therefore, I have invited two highly regarded style jumpers to share their knowledge and experience with you.

Debby Schmidt, of Joliet, Illinois, is the 1974 U.S. National Women's Champion and National Women's Style Champion. She was the first woman to win a gold medal at the National Collegiate Parachute Championships, when she became Advanced Style Champion at the Thanksgiving meet in 1972. She was a member of the U.S. team that swept the 1973 A-driatic Cup in Portoroz, Yugoslavia, with a total of seven gold

109

medals (including an individual gold medal for Miss Schmidt). She was a member of the U.S. Team that competed in Szolnok, Hungary, in 1974 at the 12th World Parachuting Championships, where she finished fourth overall and fifth in style.

Air Force Lieutenant James L. Hayhurst is a 1974 graduate of the United States Air Force Academy in Colorado, where he was an active member of the Academy's parachute team. Very early in his jumping career, he was Intermediate Style Champion of the National Collegiate Parachuting League (NCPL). He placed third in style at the 1974 U.S. National Parachuting Championships with an average time of 7.94 seconds.

Charles W. Ryan

Chuck Collingwood, 1973 Style Champion and Overall Champion at the U.S. Nationals, on a style jump over Tahlequah, Oklahoma. (Photo by Joe Gonzales)

Debby Schmidt

James L. Hayhurst

The point of style is to try to complete a series of six simple maneuvers as quickly and precisely as possible. Accomplishing this can be very difficult without a set of rules to follow. These basic rules of style apply to *you*—whether you have 30, 300, or 3,000 jumps.

The most important rule in style is: *To go fast, you don't try to go fast; rather, you try to gain complete control over the series.* The key to this control is to stay tight. Ninety percent of style is staying tight.

AIR WORK

The style jump consists of a fall-away or dive followed by a style series comprising two 360-degree horizontal turns, a backloop (360-degree vertical turn), two more turns, and another backloop.

Fall-away

The fall-away is very important for building up enough speed to complete the style set quickly. There are two ways to fall away: in the style tuck or in the vertical dive. The tuck is easier to master than the dive; and with good control, you can

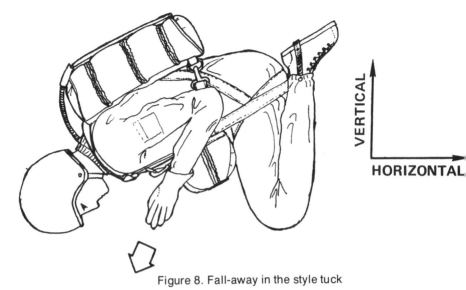

Figure 8. Fall-away in the style tuck

consistently turn in the low sevens, low sixes, or maybe faster. The key points of the fall-away position are:

1. Feet against buttocks.
2. Knees against the reserve.
3. Knees together.
4. Feet together.
5. Elbows touching the sides. (At first the forearms may be extended straight out from the sides—perpendicular to the body—for stability; but as control is mastered, the hands should be placed under the shoulders—much as they are located near the low point of a pushup—or next to the reserve.)
6. Shoulders rounded.
7. Head tucked down.
8. Body tight and rigid.
9. Mind relaxed. (The closer you get to relaxing in this foreign environment—the air—the easier it will be to concentrate.)

Figure 8 shows the fall-away in the style tuck. The time of

the fall-away should be at least 13 seconds—enough time to be sure of reaching terminal velocity. It is a serious error to attempt a maneuver before sufficient speed is built up, because a low-speed maneuver requires comparatively large body movements. (Our fall-aways last 16 to 19 seconds.) Do not go on to turns until you have mastered the fall-away.

Turns

In learning to do turns, start with body turns. Just use your body by dropping a shoulder and turning your head. Then when you use your arms, the turns will be easier, and your arms will have less tendency to "swing around" uncontrollably. When you are doing turns using your arms, the key points of the turning position are:

1. Legs up together and tight; same as the basic position.
2. Turn-side shoulder (*left* turn, *left* shoulder) dipped slightly.
3. Inside arm (*left* turn, *left* arm)
    a. Elbow against side.
    b. Forearm pointing down and out (toward the earth).
4. Outside arm and elbow (*left* turn, *right* arm) tucked in, hand near neck or face.
5. Head
    a. For beginners, tucked straight down.
    b. For experienced stylists, tucked straight down and tilted in the direction of the turn.

There is a good reason for the difference in head position. Before the jumper acquires timing or rhythm—which is gained through mental series practice (discussed later) and actual jump experience—he turns by looking at the heading on the ground. As the inexperienced jumper comes to the end of a turn, a tilted head may cause him to see the heading before his body gets to it. As a result, he will not make a full 360-degree

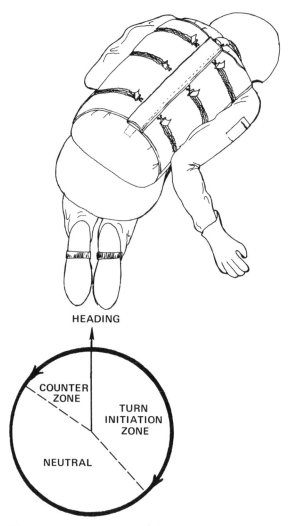

Figure 9. Right turn, shown from above, with timing

turn and will be penalized for undershooting it. (See Figure 9.)

The key points for the turning position are basic. The exact positioning of the hands varies. Each jumper must determine this for himself.

Hold the turn position for a moment, until the turn starts.

Then ease into a neutral position in preparation for the counter, transition, and following maneuvers.

The transition from turn to turn is just a turn in the opposite direction. The transition from turn to stop or from turn to backloop is a *counter* in the opposite direction.

A counter is nothing more than a *momentary turn initiation.* You start a turn in the opposite direction but resume neutral position *before* a turn in that direction begins. This will stop your rotation and leave you on heading, ready for the next maneuver.

It is important to add speed gradually to avoid losing control of the turn. At the same time, it is important to push yourself just a little past the "comfortable" stage so that you will advance. When you start a turn, be positive about your movements; don't make "wishy-washy" turns.

Backloops

When you first start learning the backloop, do it alone as a separate maneuver. Imagine pulling your knees tightly up to your chest while your arms and head are positioned as if you were doing a front dive off a diving board. This will help you picture the backloop and the muscles involved to make it work.

The key points of the backloop position (shown in Figure 10) are:

1. Legs up and tightly together, the same as the basic position.
2. Head tucked straight down.
3. Arms extended and parallel, with palms down.

Since a backloop always follows a turn, it should be practiced that way *after you master the backloop.* Before starting the backloop, you must negate the momentum that was gained from the turn. To do this, you counter the turn; that is, you initiate a turn in the opposite direction for a very brief moment.

To counter the backloop, move your arms back to the neutral position with your palms down. (If you are trying the

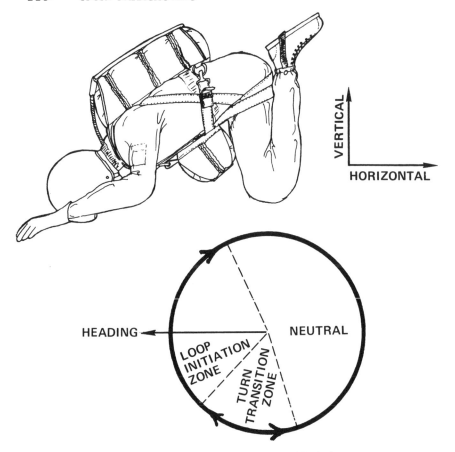

Figure 10. Backloop, side view, with timing

backloop only, you might have to bring your hands back far-ther than your original position to keep from doing several loops.)

If you plan to follow the backloop with a turn, follow the counter by *arm movement* into the position of the next turn. It is important here to *keep your head rigid*. Often a jumper who tilts his head or looks in the direction of the next turn will cause that turn to begin before the backloop is completed. This will result in an "arrow"—a penalty for sweeping into a turn before the backloop is completed.

It is very difficult but most important for you to *keep tight* during the first loop and the following turn.

Combinations

After you learn turns and backloops, start putting them together in combinations. First try turn—stop—turn—stop. Next do turn—stop—loop—stop—turn—stop. Then do turn—stop—turn—stop—loop—stop.

This last combination is a half series. Put together two half series and you will have a complete style set.

The stops should still be there whether you are turning in the sixes or sixteens, but as you gain control and speed in the maneuvers, you will also gain control and speed in the transitions. Stopping after every maneuver, even for only a split second, will teach the beginner to become controlled and penalty-free, and it will help the experienced jumper to stay that way.

If you start to have problems, *stop and go back.* Errors multiply themselves. The constant movement of style is gained through control, not blind speed. Never thrash around the sky. Don't cheat yourself. Just do "honest style."

GROUND WORK

The importance of ground work in style training is too often overlooked. It is the most important part of the style jump, yet many people don't know about it, forget it, or ignore it. The difference between ground work and no ground work is the difference between 6- to 8-second sets and 9- to 16-second sets in a relatively small number of jumps. A good background in ground work is as important in style as in flight training. Compare the pilot with 100 hours of flying time *plus* 100 hours in a Link trainer with a pilot who has 100 hours of flying time only.

We can divide ground work into three basic areas: mental, mental-physical, and physical.

Mental

This is an extremely critical part of ground work. It consists of creating a mental picture of yourself during an entire style jump. This mental picture has a rhythm or timing that can be carried into actual style. This is the rhythm we mentioned earlier. When you prepare for an actual competition style jump, your mental picture should include everything—from putting on your gear and getting into the aircraft through the opening of your parachute. A little thing like the pilot's opening the door and saying, "Exit, exit, exit!" can break your concentration if you're not expecting it. Your mental ground work will give you an excellent base from which to work when you are actually in the air.

Mental-Physical

Combine your mental series with physical simulation of your style and you have the mental-physical aspect of ground work. Kneel on a bed, lie on your back, or get into a style harness. Then go through the entire jump (at least from exit to opening) both mentally and physically. Use a stopwatch here to help you develop your timing.

Physical

This aspect of your training should be designed to help you increase your physical effectiveness in style by general physical conditioning. Key points are:

1. Strength and flexibility in your legs.
2. Strength in your stomach.
3. General physical conditioning.

The time devoted to each of these three types of ground work varies from person to person and from day to day. The importance of ground workouts cannot be overemphasized. Develop a program and stick to it. It will be well worth the effort.

Judge evaluates style through telemeter, noting any maneuver that requires a penalty. (USPA Photo)

THE STYLE COMPETITOR

Imagine a continuum from practice jumps to competition jumps. Professional style jumps should lie at the center of the continuum.

This is the place where a jumper can think of his practice jump as an actual competition jump and can go to a major competition and think of his jump as "just another jump," no different from any other.

Of course, the best way to achieve this state is to compete on almost every jump. But since this is impossible, mental simulation of the actual competition is the answer. The center of the continuum is where the jumper's emotional state changes least—where he is relaxed enough to take extra "risks" to attain his goal. His momentary functioning will be boosted; yet at the same time, his overall level of stress will be low enough to allow him to concentrate.

HONEST STYLE

Style is an exciting mental and physical challenge. Possibly the greatest challenge is for the competitor to accept just how simple style can be. By following the basics of air work and ground work, and by refusing to cheat yourself, you will be able to do "honest style." And honest style is *fast* style!

All the jumpers in this star hold Gold Wings, representing 1,000 freefalls. (Photo by Ray Cottingham, who has Gold Wings, too)

10

Basic Relative Work Techniques

by Pat Works

Style and accuracy are individual events in competition. Relative work is a group activity, in which two or more jumpers maneuver together in freefall to form a "star" (which is actually a circle) or some other formation or series of formations.

Relative work (RW) gets its name from the fact that the relative motion *between* jumpers is constantly varied to perform freefall maneuvers. You must change your rate of descent (falling speed) and your horizontal movement over the ground relative to other jumpers. And of course you must learn to control the direction of your flight. While you appear to be "flying" parallel to the ground, you are actually falling at various angles to the earth to achieve this apparent flight. Most jumpers have begun to learn these techniques by the time they receive the A license (at least 25 freefalls), and they must master them before they can meet the requirements for the B license (at least 50 freefalls).

Relative work is often called "fun jumping," because while

style and accuracy require lonely dedication and practice, RW can be done just for the fun of the jump and the exhilaration of controlling the flight of the body in freefall. This is not to say that RW is easy. Though a two-man hookup is relatively easy once you learn the basic maneuvers and your body's flight characteristics, the formation of large stars and sequential formations is as demanding as style or accuracy.

The high degree of skill necessary for large stars is recognized by an award called the Bob Buquor Memorial Star Crest. To earn the SCR card and patch, signifying that you are a Star Crest Recipient, you must participate in a star consisting of eight or more people. The award, named in honor of one of the pioneers in relative work and freefall photography, is coveted among relative workers. If you don't hold the SCR, you have not "arrived" in RW. Another award, the SCS, was added later. The Star Crest Soloist must enter a star eighth or later. Later versions of these awards are the Night SCR and Women's SCR, along with their SCS counterparts.

Relative work has come a long way. It is now a standard part of both national and international competition, and the Federation Aeronautique Internationale (FAI) has sanctioned World Parachuting Championships of Relative Work for odd-numbered years, starting in 1975 in West Germany. (A World Cup of Relative Work was held at Fort Bragg, North Carolina, in 1973 to test the concept of international competition in RW. It was highly successful and is now a standard part of world competition.)

As I did for the style and accuracy chapters, I have invited an expert in relative work to discuss the basic techniques of that aspect of sport parachuting.

Pat Works, who holds SCS-1, started jumping in Texas in 1961 and now has over a thousand jumps. He competed on the fourth-place 10-man team at the U.S. National Parachuting Championships in 1972. In the same year, his four-man team was ranked fifth in the nation. He has been involved in relative work competition ever since.

Mr. Works and his wife, Jan, publish RW Underground, a newsletter known throughout the world as a medium of communication that specifically promotes the growth of relative work among sport parachutists. Mr. Works' efforts were significant in helping achieve national recognition of RW on the competition level. He is a cofounder of the Relative Work Council, which serves as liaison between relative workers and the Competition Committee of the USPA.

Pat and Jan Works now live in Fullerton, California; both remain quite active in sport parachuting.

Charles W. Ryan

Pat Works

Fast-moving precision freefall relative work is the most rapidly growing aspect of sport parachuting. Parachutists like RW because it is fast and exciting, and because it feeds a hunger for learning that grows with every jump. Soon you realize that the flight of ideas is as real as the flight of freefall relative work. You're into RW!

Relative work demands teamwork as does no other aspect of sport parachuting. When done well, it's an exhilarating coordination of the senses with physical movement in harmony with others. It is among the world's greatest team sports.

RW can be compared with football. Both sports involve "plays." In the timing, symmetry, and beautifully coordinated motion of football team players, perfection is vitally important. In any football play, each man has an assignment, and the play is not successful unless each individual does his job well. Timing and teamwork are just as critical in RW.

Relative work is the closest to flying man can come using his body alone. RW *is* flying. The exultation of seeing fine relative work flying is surpassed only by the joy of being part of the jump yourself.

If you are a jumping novice interested in getting into relative work, you should be making controlled 30-second delays, and you should be able to perform (and stop) turns and dives. When you feel comfortable in the air and are able to manage unpoised, "bomb out the door" type exits, you are ready to start learning RW.

Begin with two-man hookups, then three-man stars, with experienced relative workers who can answer your questions, correct your mistakes, and watch your progress. You will be expected to demonstrate ability at the two-, three-, and four-man levels before you can hope to start working on larger stars.

Most RW novices grossly overrate their own RW skill. Before embarking on large-star relative work, analyze your situation. A realistic self-assessment of your actual RW proficiency level is the best step. Can you come in third or fourth 90 per-

The two-man hookup is the first step in the progression to large-star relative work. (Photo by Ralph White)

Two-woman hookup. (Photo by Tom Schapanski)

cent of the time on small star loads? If not, you lack the real qualifications for big star loads, where the mental tension you place on yourself will degrade your RW performance to an unacceptable level.

Check your logbook. Divide your total number of RW jumps into your total of *successful* RW jumps. The resulting percentage will give you an idea of your skill level. If it is less than 80 percent, you need more small-star RW practice.

An RW Skill Test

The following RW skill test can be applied to determine your rate of progress. It is also excellent practice. Perform the described maneuvers on 30-second delays. Start with the easiest, moving on to more difficult maneuvers as you achieve the recommended proficiency:

Level	Maneuvers	Recommended Proficiency
1	Make contact with a novice who is making controlled 30-second delays. Novices are hard to catch, since their RW skill is low.	90%
2	Make a two-man hookup with another RW novice; then break off, turn 360 degrees; make another hookup. Repeat for a third hookup. (Three separate hookups from 7,200 feet.)	80%
3	Two-man hookup, backloop; second hookup, backloop; third hookup. (Three separate hookups from 7,200 feet.)	75%
4	Three-man star, backloop, another three-man star, all on same jump from 7,200 feet.	70%
5	Delay your exit from 1 to 3 seconds and still enter, or pin, cleanly from 7,200 feet.	80%

6   Be part of a four-man star built   65%
     in 12 seconds or less.

If you are proficient at these maneuvers, your RW skill will speak a lot more convincingly than your mouth, and you'll find yourself on more and more large-star loads as your skill progresses.

If you happen to be a nervous novice, here are some hints that may help you on large-star loads.

Which Exit Position?

When you first start doing RW from aircraft larger than you are used to, spend at least two jumps going last and not trying to get in. Just get the feel of the aircraft, the exit, tracking, etc. When you are comfortable, try to go out fourth, fifth, or sixth.

The "Murphy's Star" is one of the official formations in four-man sequential relative work. (Photo by Ray Cottingham)

Relative workers leave C-46 over Sylvania, Georgia. (Photo by Andy Keech)

The reason is simple. You'll be a bit too nervous to handle the base, (first person in star), pin (second person into star), or third positions properly, and these are the key to the whole jump. If you are in one of these positions, the star load depends on your getting in when you're supposed to. That's pressure you don't need.

Going out seventh or later involves too much diving, tracking, and high-speed approaches—and not enough close-in RW and star-flying.

Going in the middle of the load gives you a lot of time to make a good, leisurely, skillful approach and entry. It also gives you a margin for error so you can reapproach if you miss your first try.

Discipline Yourself

No one expects you to be perfect right from the start. However, everyone does rightfully expect you to act sensibly and to place the integrity of the star above your own desire to "get in," to "be faster," or similar ego trips. If you do a good job and give it a well-controlled try, you'll be asked on more loads even if you don't always get in.

But bomb the star, approach too hot, go below and loiter there, and you'll build a bad reputation long before you build a star. Exhibit self-control.

When you do get on a big RW load, listen closely to the star-master. You will be judged on your ability to follow directions. He will give you a flying assignment that you are expected to carry out.

Dig the sky and the clouds on the ride up. Clear your mind, get your will under control. Build a mental picture of what you are about to do, and then concentrate on achieving a relaxed attitude about it.

Making Your Exit

Making your first several exits for big-star work can be unsettling. Exits are hard to control. If you let yourself get rattled by a bad exit, the rest of your jump reflects that state of mind. So do yourself a favor and remember that the exit is just part of a whole sequence of things.

Get solidly into the exit lineup. Concentrate on getting into the count and sway of it. First work on just getting out the door. If you hit the door jamb or "Z" out the door, resolve not to panic or overcompensate (overamp) on the rest of the jump.

When you find yourself outside the aircraft in the unfamiliar subterminal air, you'll have a tendency to "fight it" in your efforts to get squared away quickly. But if you *stiffen* your mind and body to regain control, you'll lose the relaxed edge required for the rest of the jump.

Relaxing your entire body is the answer. Your arms, legs, and torso will automatically find your flight path for you, just

Ten-man team piles out of C-46 over Zephyrhills, Florida. (Photo by Andy Keech)

as feathers find it for a dart or an arrow. And by not rushing to "catch up," you'll likely find that your entry time will be respectable anyway.

If you lose sight of the star because you've Z-ed out, don't get frantic. Relax. Go into a shallow dive, find the others on your load who are making a beeline for the star, and follow them.

The Approach

As you're aiming at the star, plan to stop dead still at a spot about 30 feet outside the star and off to one side, at a point about 15 to 20 feet above the level of the star. Stop dead still, then make a final approach and dock to enter.

The reason for stopping is important. As a novice, you don't have enough experience to know when you're in "full stop" in

Pat Works (upper left) makes final approach to building star. (Photo by Andy Keech)

In the slot and on the wrists. (Photo by Ray Cottingham)

relation to the star. You'll tend to see movement as coming from the *star* and not from yourself. You have to *stop* to be sure—at least for your first few attempts. Otherwise you'll end up sliding around the star, and you could bomb it—or someone near it.

You aim to the side of the star for the same reason. If you aim directly at the star and misjudge your stopping point by 10 feet, you'll likely sail right through the star. Maybe you won't hit anyone. Maybe you will.

If you stop 15 to 20 feet above the star, you'll retain some altitude to convert back into forward momentum to make a forceful and precise final approach without undue effect from the "burble," or wall of turbulent air around the star.

If you find yourself stuck in a slot and unable to lay your hands on wrists, going stiff and reaching for them won't help. You must flare up and back out of the slot so you can swoop in again with enough momentum to carry you onto the wrists. You'll need to back at least 8 feet out and 6 feet up to attempt a reapproach.

Docking and Entry

As a novice, touching wrists will at first send such a charge of adrenalin through you that you'll probably stiffen, float, and mess up.

When you dock on wrists or wherever, do not do anything else until you relax and settle to fly *with* the star. A premature entry can endanger the star. A slow, careful entry affects nothing except the traffic of others waiting to get in behind you.

When you have a good, solid grip on a wrist or jumpsuit and are flying with the star, shake and break to enter. Now relax and dig it. (But while you're relaxed, don't forget that you still have to help fly the star.)

Those already in the star break only when the entering jumper has a firm grip. (Photo by Ray Cottingham)

Breakoff and Pull

At breakoff time, ALWAYS make a 180-degree turn and track (move horizontally) *away* from the star until opening (pull) time. To pull early, or fail to track away, or to track for the spot (where you will open your chute) can easily get you hurt or killed. A large percentage of RW-related injuries occur because of failure to properly clear the contact area.

At pull time, ALWAYS give a waveoff and check around and above you before pulling. Do not sit up to pull, because you will backslide toward the contact area and a possible collision.

Do not pull above 3,500 feet. Pulling higher on an RW load is dangerous and marks you as a nitwit. Pulling higher means everyone has to stop doing RW and worry about an open canopy in the area.

If someone in your area dumps while you are still in freefall, dive away from him immediately. If you've missed his body and canopy, wait until he gets line stretch before you pull. If you pull before he gets full line stretch, you could end up eating canopy. Remember that most canopies surge forward at peak opening pressure.

Once you have inflation, check around you for other open canopies. Have your hands on the toggles. Be ready to make a quick turn to avoid an entanglement.

Doing all this is not hard if you've preconditioned yourself on other jumps and on the ground. The important thing to remember about proper breakoff and pull procedures for RW is that you *do* them.

After the Jump

Don't expect everyone to feel the same way about the jump as you do. Some will be happy with their performance; others will be down because they feel they flew like a turkey (performed poorly). Only about a third of the jumpers will actually have seen what went on, and most of those will disagree on some points.

It's a good idea to listen to what everyone on the load has to say. If *you* don't have anything positive to say, then *say nothing.* If you cannot come across with good vibes, then keep the negative things to yourself. Don't spit in the soup that you'll have to eat later.

If you made a serious mistake on the jump you'll know it, of course, and you'll hear about it. But if you did okay, or didn't do as well as you had wished and don't know why, then wait a bit, try to remember accurately everything that happened, and talk it over with one of the more experienced RWers who was on the load.

Jumping with a Team

As you gain more experience, you may decide to jump with a team, whether it be for serious competition or just for the security of always having a group of people to jump with.

Jumping with a team can be a very rewarding experience. You can learn much about RW by jumping with the same people most of the time—they'll be a constant against which you can practice your flying techniques. You'll be able to see more clearly, jump after jump, what your body is actually doing in relation to the others.

Every team jump is planned in advance. You'll take your assigned place in the lineup on jump run, and your exit will be better because of your familiarity with the count and sway of the team.

Outside the plane, you'll always know where the star is and what your flight pattern should be. You'll be familiar with the falling speed of the star so that your flare point (point at which you change your position to slow down) is not a matter of guesswork.

In the star, you'll feel the charge of good vibes that flows around the circle when you all know it's a good jump. The electricity of a team trying its best to work together to build a fast star or an intricate formation is very exciting.

And should your team go into competition, you'll have the

Photographing relative workers also has its problems as freefall photographer Andy Keech demonstrates as he gets ready to go to work. (Photo by Jerry Irwin)

pride and joy of demonstrating your hard-earned skill against others with the same interests. You are a highly tuned athlete. And you're doing what you most love to do . . . to fly.

"Look with your understanding, find out what you already know, and you'll see the way to fly."

—Jonathan Livingston Seagull

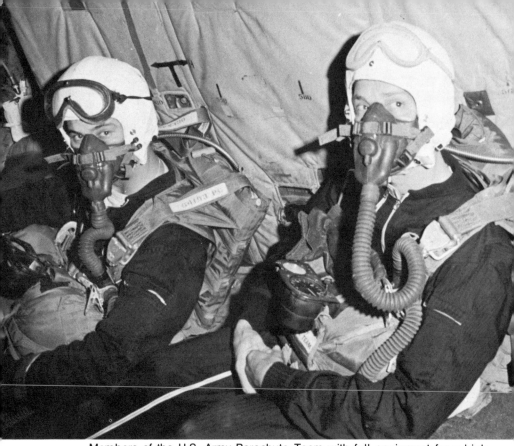

Members of the U.S. Army Parachute Team with full equipment for a high altitude jump. (Photo by Joe Gonzales)

High-Altitude Jumps

Few sport parachutists venture into the upper reaches of the atmosphere, partly because of the additional hazards, partly because of the increased expense, and mostly because of the problems of obtaining adequately equipped aircraft and special high-altitude equipment. In addition, the average jumper is either unwilling or unable to use the time and effort necessary for the special training that is absolutely essential for safe high-altitude jumps.

"High altitude" is used here to mean any altitude above 15,000 feet above sea level, but the USPA actually divides these higher altitudes into three separate classifications:

- *Intermediate altitude.* From 15,000 to 20,000 feet above sea level.
- *High altitude.* From 20,000 to 40,000 feet above sea level.
- *Extreme altitude.* Above 40,000 feet above sea level.

The environment becomes increasingly more hostile above

15,000 feet. The first hazard to become apparent is the lack of oxygen. Even at 15,000 feet, the reduced supply of oxygen to the brain impairs judgment and introduces a real element of danger. For this reason, the Basic Safety Regulations of the USPA require the sport parachutist to have supplementary oxygen above this altitude. NOTE: Not only must the oxygen supply be adequate, it must also be the *right kind* of oxygen. Medical oxygen will not do, because it has a high moisture content, and the icing of the valves of your oxygen equipment can render it useless.

Pressure steadily decreases with an increase in altitude and begins to present a problem around 25,000 feet. At this altitude, nitrogen bubbles begin to form in the bloodstream, causing "bends," or pains in the joints and muscles. Since the natural atmosphere is about 80 percent nitrogen, the bends can be prevented by getting the nitrogen out of the bloodstream. This is accomplished by breathing 100 percent oxygen for at least an hour before reaching 25,000 feet. Above an altitude of about 40,000 feet, the body cannot function properly without some kind of pressure suit.

Although not as obvious as the hazards of lower pressures and reduced oxygen, *temperature* also decreases as you go higher, until the stratosphere is reached, at which point the temperature remains fairly constant at 67° *below* zero Fahrenheit. But at much lower altitudes, merely keeping warm can be a serious problem.

Because almost no one really understands the hazards of high-altitude jumping, physiological flight training is mandatory. High altitude can be simulated in a decompression chamber. Training in this device is available at many Air Force bases throughout the country. Through an arrangement with the Federal Aviation Administration, USPA members may take this training, which familiarizes the jumper with the problems encountered at high altitudes and allows him to learn about the special equipment he must use. An important benefit of the training is that the jumper can actually experi-

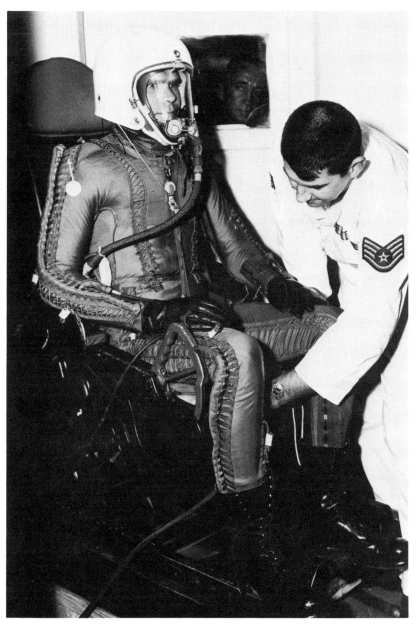

Partial pressure suit (Photo by Joe Gonzales)

PLANNING CHART for high-altitude sport parachuting

GOAL (MSL) ALTITUDE	CLASSIFI-CATION	LICENSE REQUIRED	EQUIPMENT REQUIRED * - *** - ****						PRE S
			MASK	AIRCRAFT ONBOARD OXYGEN SOURCE			BAILOUT OXYGEN SOURCE		
				REGULATOR	SETTING		For FREEFALL descent	For CANOPY descent	
					Auto-matic	Manual			H pre rec
60,000			Pressure suit helmet—integrated breathing apparatus required.						
50,000	EXTREME								
		US/FAI Class "C"			Emer-gency	Above 45M	Standard emergency "bailout bottle" assembly		
43,000						45M			P pre rec
						43M			
40,000					100% Oxygen	41M		No suitable "off the shelf" hardware available at this time.	
35,000			Positive pressure	Pressure breathing		Safety	Average duration 10 - 12 minutes.		
33,000	HIGH							Standard "bailout bottle."	
30,000			Diluter demand	Diluter demand	On Normal Oxygen				n rec
25,000						Normal Oxygen			
20,000	INTER-MEDIATE	US/FAI Class "B"	Constant flow	Continuous flow	On	On	none required	none required	n rec
15,000			Use supplemental oxygen on board above 10,000 feet MSL until exit.						
			Supplemental oxygen on board aircraft. Use above 10,000 feet MSL whenever elapsed above 8,000 feet MSL is expected to exceed 30 minutes.						
10,000	LOW								
8,000		none required							
SEA LEVEL									

*Automatic Openers are recommended as a backup system on all high-altitude jumps, due to the possibility of the parachutist's being rendered unconscious by an oxygen system failure.

**Always rehearse oxygen, communication, and exit procedures before takeoff.

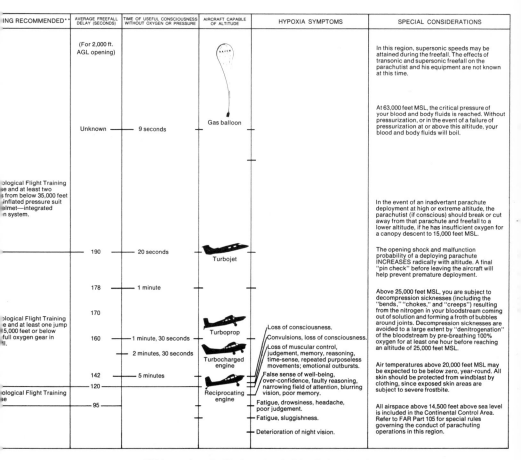

...ING RECOMMENDED**	AVERAGE FREEFALL DELAY (SECONDS)	TIME OF USEFUL CONSCIOUSNESS WITHOUT OXYGEN OR PRESSURE	AIRCRAFT CAPABLE OF ALTITUDE	HYPOXIA SYMPTOMS	SPECIAL CONSIDERATIONS
	(For 2,000 ft. AGL opening)				In this region, supersonic speeds may be attained during the freefall. The effects of transonic and supersonic freefall on the parachutist and his equipment are not known at this time.
	Unknown — 9 seconds		Gas balloon		At 63,000 feet MSL, the critical pressure of your blood and body fluids is reached. Without pressurization, or in the event of a failure of pressurization at or above this altitude, your blood and body fluids will boil.
...ological Flight Training ...e and at least two ...s from below 35,000 feet ...inflated pressure suit ...elmet—integrated ...n system.					In the event of an inadvertant parachute deployment at high or extreme altitude, the parachutist (if conscious) should break or cut away from that parachute and freefall to a lower altitude, if he has insufficient oxygen for a canopy descent to 15,000 feet MSL.
	190 — 20 seconds		Turbojet		The opening shock and malfunction probability of a deploying parachute INCREASES radically with altitude. A final "pin check" before leaving the aircraft will help prevent premature deployment.
	178 — 1 minute				Above 25,000 feet MSL, you are subject to decompression sicknesses (including the "bends," "chokes," and "creeps") resulting from the nitrogen in your bloodstream coming out of solution and forming a froth of bubbles around joints. Decompression sicknesses are avoided to a large extent by "denitrogenation" of the bloodstream by pre-breathing 100% oxygen for at least one hour before reaching an altitude of 25,000 feet MSL.
...ological Flight Training ...e and at least one jump ...5,000 feet or below ...full oxygen gear in ...l.	170		Turboprop	Loss of consciousness.	
	160 — 1 minute, 30 seconds			Convulsions, loss of consciousness.	
	— 2 minutes, 30 seconds		Turbocharged engine	Loss of muscular control, judgement, memory, reasoning, time-sense, repeated purposeless movements; emotional outbursts.	Air temperatures above 20,000 feet MSL may be expected to be below zero, year-round. All skin should be protected from windblast by clothing, since exposed skin areas are subject to severe frostbite.
	142 — 5 minutes			False sense of well-being, over-confidence, faulty reasoning, narrowing field of attention, blurring vision, poor memory.	
...ological Flight Training ...e	120		Reciprocating engine	Fatigue, drowsiness, headache, poor judgement.	All airspace above 14,500 feet above sea level is included in the Continental Control Area. Refer to FAR Part 105 for special rules governing the conduct of parachuting operations in this region.
	95			Fatigue, sluggishness.	
				Deterioration of night vision.	

***Minimum equipment listed. Equipment shown for higher altitudes satisfies all requirements for use at lower altitudes.

****Oxygen systems for high-altitude flight and parachuting should be filled with "AVIATORS" BREATHING OXYGEN, Not Medical Oxygen. Medical Oxygen has a high moisture content, which can cause oxygen mask valves to ice over in high-altitude operations.

ence hypoxia (lack of oxygen) and other physical effects of high-altitude flying.

Any sport parachutist who wishes to make a high-altitude jump should undergo the flight physiological training within a year of the planned jump.

Another problem of high-altitude jumping is that winds greatly increase in velocity with altitude. Thus, careful planning requires that you find out what the predicted winds are at every level up to jump altitude (available from Flight Service Stations and other aviation weather agencies) and take these winds into consideration in planning your exit point. If you do not do this, you might luck out and land in an open field; but you might also land in the middle of a city. In either case, you are likely to find yourself miles from the planned landing point—an inconvenience at best.

A final hazard of high-altitude jumping is that the body reaches a much higher falling speed at higher altitudes. This speed, at 40,000 feet, is about twice the usual falling speed at "normal" altitudes—120 mph. If you attain a high falling speed and pull your ripcord (or if your parachute is accidentally opened) before the denser atmosphere slows you down, you risk severe injury or even death from the opening shock.

USPA Part 115, *High Altitude Doctrine,* thoroughly covers most of the hazards of high-altitude jumping and specifies in detail the special equipment required. It also includes the planning chart reproduced in this chapter.

Before you attempt a high-altitude jump, know what the hazards are and prepare for them by obtaining good training and necessary equipment. But remember that equipment can fail. You can be rendered unconscious by lack of oxygen or immobilized by freezing temperatures. So here is a last and extremely important word: *Use an automatic opener.* It gives you an added margin of safety that could save your life.

12

Water Jumps

Because drowning accounted for a large number of parachuting fatalities in the early years of sport parachuting, a briefing on unintentional water landings is now a requirement for the A license, the first license a parachutist achieves. The briefing, conducted by a USPA Instructor/Examiner, USPA Instructor, or the student's Area Safety Officer, is intended to teach the student how to prepare for the water landing, how to enter the water, and how to get clear of his equipment (a deadly hazard) once he is in the water.

But there can be no substitute for the actual experience of landing in water with full parachute equipment, so a requirement for the D (Expert) license is an *intentional* water jump, which is performed with flotation gear and with pickup boats standing by in the water.

USPA Part 113, at the end of this chapter, provides the best guidance currently available for the safe performance of this enjoyable and instructive parachuting activity.

145

The procedures (except for the safeguards of flotation gear and pickup boats) are exactly the same for all water jumps, whether planned or not. They cover three general areas:

1. Preparation for landing in the water
2. Maneuvering the parachute for the safest entry into the water
3. Getting clear of equipment and safely out of the water

PREPARATION FOR LANDING

Once the parachutist has a good canopy over his head, he immediately begins to get ready for the water landing. If the water landing is *unintentional*, and there is any possibility at all that the jumper may land in water, *he must assume he will hit the water* and begin immediately to prepare for it. While continuing to steer his parachute to escape the water if possible, he prepares for a quick escape from his harness once he enters the water.

He unsnaps one side of the reserve belly band and swings the reserve to one side. Then he unsnaps his chest snap. (At this point, he will notice that the risers separate somewhat, but he is in no danger of falling out of the harness.) Then he pushes himself well back in the saddle, which forms a swing-like seat, and unsnaps one leg strap. (If his harness is the "split-saddle" type, he should leave *both* leg straps secure until he is in the water.)

ENTERING THE WATER

The jumper must never leave his harness until his feet are wet. Depth perception over water can be very tricky, and parachutists have been killed when what they thought was a height of only a few feet turned out to be 100 feet or more above the water.

It is of vital importance for the jumper to steer the parachute so that he is *facing into the wind* on landing. If the landing is

Water accuracy competitor hits the target as pickup canoe stands by. (Photo by Joe Gonzales)

made downwind, the canopy may remain inflated and drag the jumper *face down* in the water until he drowns. If his landing is upwind, on the other hand, his face will be out of the water, and once his leg straps are unsnapped, the inflated canopy pulls his gear *away* from him.

If the jumper follows standard procedures, he can be completely clear of all parachute gear within a couple of seconds after landing.

GETTING CLEAR AFTER LANDING

Wet nylon can be unbelievably hazardous to the jumper who does not swim clear of it immediately. (A California parachutist, a few years ago, landed in a swift irrigation canal. He got clear of the parachute and would have been safe, but he tried to save his parachute, became entangled, and drowned.)

Water jumps under careful supervision are common in the United States, because clubs sponsor them to enable parachutists to meet that requirement for a D license. The jumps are often part of a water accuracy competition.

The water jump must be carefully planned, including coordination with local, state, and federal agencies. One standing rule is that there must never be more jumpers descending under their own canopies than there are pickup boats available.

The briefing and drill for a water landing should be conducted with practice in a suspended harness. Some instructors hold a stopwatch on the parachutist in the suspended harness and require that *no more than 12 seconds* elapse for the jumper to complete his preparation for landing.

Any parachute jump made near water can become a water jump, unintentional though it may be. The USPA Basic Safety Regulations require flotation gear for all jumps made within one mile of an open body of water. Such a body of water is defined as one in which a parachutist could drown.

Conducted with proper training and under adequate supervision, the water jump is so safe that the newest holder of the A license can participate.

UNITED STATES PARACHUTE ASSOCIATION PUBLICATIONS
PART 113—DOCTRINE—WATER JUMPS, INTENTIONAL

INTRODUCTION

Water jumps are preplanned parachute jumps into an open body of water more than six (6) feet in depth. A water jump can be the easiest and safest of all parachute jumps provided normal procedures and a few additional precautions are employed. Physical injuries and drownings are almost unknown on preplanned and intentional water landings. Each year, however, there have been an unacceptable number of fatalities on accidental water entries. These deaths were due mainly to absence of flotation gear, inability to swim, use of incorrect procedures, and/or extremely cold water.

The potential always exists for unintentional water entry due to spotting error, radical wind changes, malfunctions, and landing on a reserve rather than a main. All jumps, of course, are not made on the dry home DZ. Attending meets and guest jumping at new DZs can present water obstacles not previously encountered. The technique for completely unfastening the harness prior to water entry (see para. 113.04 (a) 7.) should be taught to all jumpers should the need arise to use it, but normally the simpler method will be used. Jumpers in a

Boat crew picks up parachutist after water jump. (Photo by Joe Gonzales)

potentially dangerous descent should prepare for the eventuality of entering the water rather than devoting all their time in an effort to avoid the water obstacle. The last minute struggle to remove harness restraints when a water landing is inevitable is usually unsuccessful.

There are two major areas deserving attention. The first is the absence of depth perception over water. Unless there are objects, such as boats or familiar buoys, on the surface of the water or unless the parachutist is jumping near land, he will not be able to determine his altitude by sight alone. This peculiarity requires that the jumper maintain absolute discipline with regard to preparation for and water entry. The second area of note is the preparation and qualification of the parachutist to effectively release and clear his equipment after water entry. It is absolutely essential that persons normally jumping within one mile of an open body of water be trained in accordance with the provisions of this Part.

113.01 Qualification

(a)   Parachutists participating in water jumping should possess a currently valid Class A or higher license.

(b)   Participants should be swimmers.

(c)   Participants should have completed a comprehensive briefing and drill period within 60 days prior to the intended water jump. The training should be conducted by a USPA Club Safety Officer, USPA Area Safety Officer, USPA Instructor or Instructor/ Examiner. The instructor should enter into the jumper's log the statement "Qualified for water parachute jumping," sign his name, and indicate the date and location of the training.

113.02 Special Equipment

(a)   A U.S. Coast Guard approved flotation device.

(b)   Minimum instruments—a waterproof stopwatch is recommended for delays of more than ten (10) seconds and less than thirty (30) seconds. An altimeter should be used for delays of thirty seconds (30) or more.

(c)   Waterproof bag for instruments, if desired.

NOTE: Water will ruin an altimeter.

113.03 Training: Drill Period

(a)   Each jumper should be thoroughly briefed concerning the lack of depth perception and the techniques to assist in determining height above the water surface.

(b) Each jumper, regardless of his experience, should review procedures to properly and rapidly remove his parachute equipment. A suspended harness utilizing all personal jump equipment to be used on the actual jump, including reserve tie-down, should be used as a training device to insure complete understanding of the harness escape technique.

(c) Each jumper should be thoroughly briefed concerning the possible emergencies that may occur after water entry and the proper corrective procedures.

(d) If the jumpers wear only swimming suits, they should be aware that there will be a sharp decrease in stability and that they will fall faster. If the jumper is using a stop watch, he should shorten his delay to compensate for the increased rate of descent.

113.04 Procedures

(a) General

1. Obtain approval for the water jump from the local USPA Area Safety Officer or USPA Instructor/Examiner (BSR).

2. Check the water DZ for underwater hazards.

3. Provide no less than one recovery boat per jumper, or, if the aircraft drops one jumper per pass, one boat for every three jumpers.

4. Boat personnel should include at least one qualified parachutist and stand-by swimmer with face mask, swim fins, and experienced in life saving techniques, including resuscitation.

5. Opening altitude should not be less than 3000 feet AGL to provide ample time to prepare for water entry. This is especially true when the DZ is a small body of water and the jumper must concentrate on both accuracy and water entry.

6. The second jump run should not be made until the jumper(s) from the first pass is safely aboard the pick-up boat(s).

7. After canopy inflation:

a. In calm conditions with readily accessible pick-up boats the best procedure is simply to inflate the flotation gear and concentrate on landing in the proper area, thus preventing any possibility of falling out of the harness during attempts to unfasten leg straps, take off reserve, etc. Although there is a tendency for the jumper to become entangled in the canopy and suspension lines after landing, the flotation device will prevent the jumper from being pulled below the surface.

b. In strong winds, choppy water conditions, in competitive water jump events, or if the flotation gear cannot be inflated, separation from equipment after water entry is essential, and the following procedures apply:

(1)   Determine the angle of drift towards the target area.

(2)   Unfasten belly band on front mounted reserve.

(3)   Slide saddle forward underneath buttocks to form a seat.

(4)   Unfasten one side of the reserve. NOTE: Some parachutists may want to remove the instruments of the complete reserve and encase in a waterproof bag.

(5)   Unfasten leg straps. (Both leg straps must remain fastened on split saddle harness.)

(6)   Unfasten chest strap.

A rubber raft is sometimes used as a target during competition in connection with a water jump. (Photo by Ward Sharrer)

(7) Upon entering the water, slide forward out of the harness.

NOTE: If the underarm Air Force type (LPU) flotation equipment is used, the bladders inflate outside of the harness (although worn underneath) and removal of the harness is not practical without deflation of the bladders. If the harness must be removed after water entry when using such flotation gear, the bladders should be deflated, extricated from the harness, and reinflated (orally) one at a time.

(b) Jumpmaster Safety Checks and Briefings:
   1. USPA Parts 114 and 120 should be reviewed.
   2. Boat and Ground Crew Briefings.
      a. Communications Procedures (smoke-radio-buoys-boats)
      b. Wind Limitations
      c. Jump Order
      d. Control of Spectators and other Boats
      e. Setting up the Target
      f. Maintenance of Master Log
      g. Marking the Landing Point of the Wind Drift Indicator
      h. How to Approach Jumper and Canopy in the Water (Direction, Proximity)

Ripcord pull time on a night jump. Note helmet-mounted light. (Photo by Joe Gonzales)

13

Night Jumps

Night jumps, like water jumps, are carefully controlled because they present additional hazards to the parachutist. The handicap of reduced visibility is obvious: the world looks different without the familiar daytime landmarks, the problem of selecting the correct point of exit from the aircraft is no small matter, and depth perception is nonexistent. With the increased popularity of night relative work, involving more and more jumpers in freefall together, there is the additional hazard of a mid-air collision.

Night jumps are an enjoyable new dimension to sport parachuting, but the jumper who attempts one without adequate planning can find it more of an adventure than he bargained for. USPA Part 112, representing the best guidance currently available, is presented at the end of this chapter.

A safe night jump requires comprehensive training within 60 days of the planned jump, as well as special equipment, both on the jumper and on the ground.

Federal regulations require that the parachutist be equipped with a light *visible for three miles.* The USPA Basic Safety Regulations are even stricter, requiring a *flashing* light. The light is generally mounted on the helmet.

The parachutist needs the helmet light, a flashlight to check his canopy after opening, and a lighted altimeter. Ground lighting must be provided both to mark the target and to indicate the "spot," or point of exit from the aircraft.

The night jump, when performed according to established rules, is quite safe. Those arranging night jumps usually add even more to the margin of safety by scheduling the jump for a full moon. A night jump, including *freefall* of at least 20 seconds' duration, is a requirement for the D (Expert) license. The USPA requires that the parachutist hold at least a B license (whose requirements include 50 freefall jumps).

If you have never made a night jump, an interesting and valuable experience awaits you. But be sure you carefully plan for it and follow the established rules of safety.

UNITED STATES PARACHUTE ASSOCIATION PUBLICATIONS
PART 112—DOCTRINE—NIGHT JUMPS

INTRODUCTION

Night jumps are those made in the period between one hour after official sunset and one hour before official sunrise. Night jumps can be challenging, educational, and just plain fun, but they require additional pretraining and increased vigilance. A considerable reduction of vision poses certain problems. Overcoming these problems is what makes night jumping interesting, and your first night jump is one that you will remember for a long while. It must be kept in mind that not only does night jumping place increased requirements on the jumper, but also the pilot, jumpmaster and ground crew.

112.01 Qualifications
(a)   Parachutists participating in night jumping should possess a currently valid Class B or higher license.

(b)   Participants should have completed a comprehensive briefing and drill period within 60 days prior to the intended night

Building a night star. (Photo by M. Anderson Jenkins)

jump. The training should be conducted by a USPA Club Safety Officer, Area Safety Officer, Instructor or Instructor/Examiner. The instructor should enter into the jumper's log the statement "Qualified for night parachute jumping," sign his name, and indicate the date and location of the training.

112.02 Special Equipment

(a)   Lighted instruments (altimeter and stopwatch recommended)

(b)   Flashlight (to check canopy)

(c)   A flashing light visible for 3 miles (for protection from aircraft)

(d)   Clear goggles (if goggles are used)

(e)   Fire prevention equipment; (e.g., fire extinguisher, shovels, and sufficient personnel)

(f)   Jumper manifest (essential)

(g)   Transportation in case of fires, injuries, etc.

(h)   Target lighting equipment: Ten electrical lights (open light bulbs or flashlights) or ten 15-20 minute road flares under the direct control of individual ground crew members. WARNING: Open fires such as flare pots, cans of kerosene, or unattended road flares are extremely hazardous and should not be used.

112.03 Training

(a)   Every parachutist regardless of his experience, should participate in night jump training to learn or review:

1. Techniques of resisting disorientation

2. Use of lighted instruments, flashlight, and flashing caution light

3. Target lighting

4. Ground to air communications

5. Reserve activation

6. Use of topographical map or photograph with FAA Flight Service weather information for appropriate altitude and surface winds to compute final approach compass heading, exit, and opening point.

(b)   As with all phases of parachuting, night jumping is made safe through:

1. Special training

2. Suitable equipment

3. Preplanning

4. Good judgment

112.04 **Procedures**

(a)   General:

1. Night jumps challenge the parachutist with a new and unusual situation that must be approached with caution because:

a. There is increased likelihood of disorientation

b. The earth's surface takes on a new appearance, and familiar reference points are not available.

c. The visual senses are greatly impaired by darkness and reduction of depth perception. Be thoroughly familiar with night vision problems.

2. Parachutists infrequently make night jumps, and are less familiar with and less proficient in handling themselves under the conditions of this new environment.

3. Local Area Safety Officers or USPA Instructor/Examiners should be consulted for guidance and clearance for conducting night jumps.

NOTE: Since the parachutist cannot perceive what is taking place around him as rapidly and easily as in daylight, the time it takes for him to react to each situation will be increased. Night jumps should not be conducted in other than optimum weather conditions (e.g., light winds, good visibility).

4. Clear with state and local officials as required.

(b)   Target Configuration:

1. Arrange the lights in a circle around the target area at a radius of twenty-five meters from center.

2. Turn out the light closest to the wind line on the upwind side of the target to indicate to the jumpers the proper direction of approach. This will appear as an open doorway to the descending parachutist. If desired for greater assistance, a line of 3 or 4 lights may be placed on the wind line on the approach side of the target.

3. If night accuracy is to be performed, place a red light at dead center, protected by a plexiglass cover flush with the surface.

4. Extinguish all lights in the event of adverse weather or

other hazardous jump conditions to indicate no drop. Ground to air radio communications should be available.

(c)   Night Spotting:

1. Application of current wind information and compensation for forecast winds, surface and aloft, is critical at night. Jumpmasters should familiarize themselves with the drop zone and surrounding area in-flight during daylight, noting ground points that will display lights at night and their relationship to the drop zone and any hazardous areas. The jumpmaster should plan to use both his own visual spotting and aircraft instruments to assure accurate positioning of the aircraft.

2. During climbout, conduct a night orientation to familiarize each jumper with the night landmarks surrounding the drop zone.

3. Wind drift indicator: Several methods are available for ascertaining drift and determining the best opening point. The method described here has been found to be very satisfactory.

a. The night WDI should consist basically of a vane type pilot chute with a small hole cut in the crown to reduce oscillation.

(1)   A battery operated light which has either a lens at each end or a 360 degree lens should be suspended below the pilot chute.

(2)   Additional weights should be attached to the pilot chute to attain the proper rate of descent. The weight of the WDI may best be adjusted during daylight hours by dropping it simultaneously with a conventional paper streamer.

b. This night WDI should be used in the conventional manner.

c. The impact point of the night WDI should be marked with a readily visible light, preferably a flashing beacon, of a color contrasting with the target lights.

d. The exit point should be calculated in the conventional manner. The exit point may also be marked by some type of illumination, but if both the WDI impact point and the jumper's exit point are marked, it should be done in a contrasting manner and well known to the jumpmaster.

(d)   Jumpmaster Safety Checks and Briefings:

1. Review USPA Parts 114 and 120

(e)   Night Relative Work:

1. Night relative work requires extreme care and a minimum number of parachutists should perform relative work during a single jump. Parachutists should preplan night relative work carefully and not allow last minute deviations to interfere with safety.

2. Night relative work jumps should not be conducted from an altitude less than 7,000 feet above the surface.

3. Break-off altitude should be 3,500 feet above the surface. Maximum horizontal displacement between jumpers should be attained after breakoff, maneuvers to be only those necessary to attain maximum horizontal displacement.

WARNING: Road and other flares exude hot melted chemicals while burning and are hazardous when used by parachutists in free fall. In addition, the bright glare greatly increases the possibility of disorientation.

The Golden Knights display a flag in freefall during a Fourth of July demonstration. (Photo by Edward M. Parrish courtesy of the Army Parachute Team)

14

Demonstration Jumps

Sport parachuting (usually called "skydiving" on the posters and advance notices) has become as much a part of the air show as the aerobatics and almost as common at fairs and other outdoor festivities as the baseball pitch and the ferris wheel.

Most experienced jumpers will eagerly participate in a demonstration (exhibition) jump at any opportunity. Perhaps it is the "ham" in all of us, but to most jumpers, the "demo" jump is both a lot of fun and a challenge. The demonstration jump is a challenge because the target area is usually quite small and surrounded by obstructions: buildings, power lines, streets crowded with automobiles, and often water. Thus, care must be taken in judging the winds at altitude, choosing the exit point, and maneuvering the parachute into the landing area.

Aside from the hazards involved in missing the target, failure to land in the assigned area is damaging to the image of sport parachuting in the minds of the spectators.

163

PLANNING THE DEMO JUMP

A good demo jump requires careful planning that starts well in advance of the scheduled date. Planning (involving some paperwork) includes:

- Coordination with the FAA
- Coordination with state and local agencies
- The demonstration jump

FAA

Federal Aviation Regulations, Part 105, *Parachute Jumping*, includes one section that specifically applies to demonstration jumps. Here is the key paragraph to Section 105.15:

> No person may make a parachute jump, and no pilot in command of an aircraft may allow a parachute jump to be made from that aircraft, over or into a congested area of a city, town, or settlement, or an open air assembly of persons unless a certificate of authorization for that jump has been issued under this section. However, a parachutist may drift over that congested area or open air assembly with a fully deployed and properly functioning parachute if he is at a sufficient altitude to avoid creating a hazard to persons and property on the ground.

Since it is hard to think of a demonstration jump that does not fall within the specifications of FAR 105.15, it is absolutely necessary that you obtain the required authorization for the jump. J. Scott Hamilton, a National Director of USPA, Chairman of the Safety and Training Committee, and an attorney with special training in aviation law, writes:

> Where the regs require authorization, the FAA has pretty broad discretion to grant or refuse to grant a Certificate of Authorization, and bureaucrats are notoriously reluctant to sign their name to anything *permitting* anyone to do anything as crazy as jumping out of an airplane in flight. Thus, you'd better have ALL of your paperwork in order when you *first* present it to the GADO, and you'd better be prepared to follow it up with tenacious pressure and reasoned arguments why there's no danger to "persons and

property on the ground" (a favorite FAA phrase) and why they had best quit giving you the runaround and issue the Certificate (this may include having your lawyer give them an inquiring telephone call).

Finally it should be noted that where the jump is to be made onto an airport, FAA regulations also require that permission of the Airport Manager be obtained. You'd better get it in writing, too, because if anything goes wrong, he could change his story in a flash, otherwise. If this sounds like a lot of trouble, it is. Setting up exhibition jumps is one of the most exasperating of human endeavors, and you can bet that if you successfully run the regulatory maze and get everything in order, a typhoon will strike the moment you turn in on jump run. (*Parachutist*, May 1973.)

The "GADO" in Hamilton's statement means the General Aviation District Office controlling the location of the demo jump. A recent reorganization of the FAA has resulted in the renaming of some GADOs as Flight Standards District Office (FSDO), which is a kind of super-GADO. However, the procedure is the same in either case.

Hamilton's pessimism is well-founded, because each GADO is, for all practical purposes, a law unto itself. Many GADOs are noted for their cooperation with local sport parachutists and almost never refuse to authorize a reasonably planned demo jump. Others are notorious for rarely authorizing *any* exhibition jump, regardless of the competence of the jumpers.

The Certificate of Authorization is obtained via the FAA Form 400, which should be submitted in *triplicate* early enough for coordination by FAA with interested controlling agencies, such as an Air Route Traffic Control Center or a control tower.

To be safe, the form should be received by the applicable GADO or FSDO at least two weeks in advance of the jump. The form can be submitted to any GADO or FSDO and then forwarded to the office that has jurisdiction, but time is saved by submitting it to the proper office in the first place.

If the demonstration jump is part of an air show, clearance with FAA is usually handled by the person arranging the entire event, but *check on this point to be sure.* Otherwise, you may find that you have to either cancel your jump or risk stiff penalties from the federal authorities.

The GADO or FSDO prefers that interested controlling agencies be contacted in advance of submitting the Form 400, and verbal approvals obtained. These verbal approvals are noted as attachments to the Form 400, and copies of the paperwork are sent out to those controlling agencies by the GADO or FSDO.

If the demonstration jump is near or in controlled air space (and most are), several different agencies may want to know about the jump. A telephone call to GADO is usually necessary to find out which agencies. This depends on the location of the jump and the desired jump altitudes.

In the case of a jump I arranged into Foster City, California (in the Oakland Bay Area), verbal approval was obtained from Bay Traffic Control and San Carlos Tower. This jump, into a

Bob Myatt, Glenn Bhonen, and Bob Arnold on jump run for a demonstration jump at Bremerhaven, Germany. (Photo by Heinz Mueller)

softball field bounded on one side by the bay and in an area of very heavy commercial air traffic, was approved with no difficulty at all, as are most exhibition jumps in the Bay Area. If such a jump can be approved, there is no good reason why any well-planned jump should be disapproved, but GADOs vary.

Any pertinent information, including verbal approvals, should be provided as attachments to the Form 400. A *map* of the jump area should certainly be included.

In obtaining verbal approvals, the exact time or times of jumps must be specified, and all altitudes (including that of the wind drift pass of the airplane over the target to drop a wind drift indicator) must be given. If there is a change in the time or jump altitude, interested agencies must be contacted for another approval.

Only pilot(s) and aircraft listed on the Form 400 may be used for the jump unless the change is approved by the GADO. If *any* unauthorized change is made in pilot or aircraft, the jump is illegal.

If a change is necessary after the Form 400 has been submitted, it can usually be made by telephone to the controlling GADO.

The FAA requires not only authorization but *notification*. A Notice to Airmen (NOTAM) must be filed with the controlling Flight Service Station in advance of the jump or jumps. The NOTAM should be filed about 5 days in advance and confirmed by telephone a few hours in advance of the jump.

But the NOTAM is not enough. The pilot must advise the applicable agency by radio *at least 5 minutes* before each exit of jumpers from the aircraft. The same 5-minute notice must be given before the wind drift pass.

State and Local Agencies

While the airspace is controlled by the FAA, you must *land* in an area under the control of various state and local agencies. It should be obvious that written permission of the landowner must be obtained in advance, but you will have to check out other state and local regulations.

Some states, such as California and New York, have extensive regulations governing parachuting. Because of the exhaustive safeguards inherent in federal regulations, there is no additional regulation in most states, but the trend is toward more overlapping state control. Be sure you know what the regulations are in your state and comply with them to the letter.

A statement is often required from the pertinent city, county, or state agency giving approval of the jump. Such local approvals, where applicable, must be obtained before the FAA will authorize the jump. Usually there will be no objection if the phrase "so long as such activity conforms to federal, state, and local rules and regulations" is included. Some public agencies will not issue a letter of *authorization* for a parachute jump, for various reasons. If this is not attainable, a written statement of "no objection" is usually acceptable.

Since flares are normally used in connection with exhibition jumps, the local fire department should be notified. Notification to the local law enforcement agency is also prudent.

Arrangements are simplified if the group contracting for the jump is asked to obtain the property owner's permission and to notify the law enforcement agency and fire department.

THE DEMONSTRATION JUMP

Remember that the demonstration jump is a show. It must please the crowd. If it does not, you will not please the sponsors, and you are not likely to be invited back.

Your planned "show" will depend on the number of jumpers available and the number of separate jumps planned. Bear in mind that while relative work involving several jumpers may be fun for you, it will do nothing for the spectators unless they can both *see* and *understand* what is happening.

Jumpers often use smoke flares for demonstration jumps. (Photo by Andy Keech)

Diamond formation with smoke flares. (Photo courtesy of the Army Parachute Team)

Smoke flares are usually used in demo jumps, because it is easy for spectators to see smoke trails, whose patterns in the sky are often striking, while the jumpers themselves are often mere dots, if they can be seen at all.

If only one load of jumpers is to be used, it is often a good idea for one jumper to go out at a fairly low altitude to get the attention of the crowd while the other jumpers climb to a higher altitude. (A flag jump is especially effective during the Fourth of July holiday, a time of peak demand for exhibition jumps.)

If several jumps are planned, relative work at altitude (with smoke flares) may be combined with a minimum-altitude "stack" of individually exiting jumpers. Surprising as it may seem to many parachutists, the most effective part of a demo jump, from the viewpoint of the spectators, may be the lower-altitude jumps that allow the crowd to see the jumpers as they leave the aircraft and open their parachutes. This they can understand.

For any exhibition that is not obvious to spectators, a narrator on the ground is essential. This person, who should be an experienced jumper, can tell the crowd what to expect and describe what is happening during every phase of the demonstration. Do not leave this task to the MC at an air show that includes other events. He probably won't know much more than the spectators, and all of your planning might be wasted.

Your planning must include a ground crew. Ground winds can be notoriously variable, so someone on the ground should pop smoke flares so the jumpers know what the ground wind direction is during the descent under the canopies.

Since things often look a lot different at altitude, the landing area should be marked with brightly colored panels or some other highly visible device.

Any planning of a demo jump into a "tight" area should include a preplanned escape route. The wind could shift, or you might have to ride your reserve down if your main malfunctions, so you might find yourself unable to reach the planned

Bob Myatt jumps into the Volksfest at Bremerhaven, Germany. (Photo by Heinz Mueller)

landing area. Failure to reach the target hurts the demonstration, but failure to plan for alternate landing areas can hurt *you*.

The landing area should be roped off or otherwise kept clear of spectators. Spectators, especially children, will try to get to the landing area, and you might find your target covered with people—a hazard to both the spectators and yourself.

The demonstration is not over when you land, because you are still on display. Thus, it is important that all parachutists involved dress and act in a manner that is a credit to sport parachuting.

Your primary reason for making a demonstration jump may be the fun of the jump itself or the money it makes for yourself or for your club, but the jump has other aspects. Most of the spectators know little about sport parachuting. What they see will affect the way *they* feel about *your* sport. Be sure that everything you do works to the advantage of sport parachuting.

Not the least of considerations is the fact that those spectators are also voters, and they can influence the people who make the regulations governing sport parachuting.

Plan a pleasing demonstration and execute it competently and safely. If you do, you won't have to worry about the image you create.

USPA Part 118, *Demonstration Jumps*, gives detailed information that should be required reading for anyone planning to participate in a demonstration jump.

15

Equipment

A subject of obvious importance to the sport parachutist, starting with his first jump, is his equipment. The beginning jumper has very little interest in his specific equipment beyond his hope and expectation that it is safe; that is, that the parachute will open properly and let him down safely. At any reputable drop zone, which means the great majority, he need not worry about this.

In the beginning, the problem of choosing his equipment is out of the student's hands. He uses what is provided for him, and in most cases this is surplus equipment. It is used, and it probably doesn't look very pretty.

If you are thinking of getting into sport parachuting, don't make the mistake of comparing your equipment with that of experienced jumpers. Their equipment probably looks very different from your own. Much of it is beautiful, stylishly designed, and impressive in appearance. But pretty is not the same as safe, and the rig you use for your first jump might actually be safer than some of the custom rigs you see.

Student on his first freefall exits over New Hanover, Pennsylvania, as the aircraft is reflected on his helmet. (Photo by Jerry Irwin)

Most beginning jumpers make only two or three jumps; a small percentage go on to licensing. If you are one of that tiny group, you will reach a point when you want to think about buying your own equipment instead of renting it.

This chapter is intended for anyone who wants to buy his own equipment, whether he has 10 jumps or several hundred.

MAJOR COMPONENTS OF THE PARACHUTE

From the very beginning, you should be learning as much about the parachute as you can. In a very few jumps, you will be packing your own main parachute (an FAA-certificated

An equipment check should precede every jump. (Photo by Steven L. Waterman)

rigger packs your reserve), and before long you will be totally responsible for insuring the safety of your equipment.

There are six main components of the sport parachute:

- Pilot chute
- Deployment device
- Canopy
- Ripcord (or static line)
- Container
- Harness

Pilot Chute

As the name implies, this is a small parachute, constructed in the same manner as the main canopy and of similar material, whose purpose is to initiate deployment of the main parachute. Standard pilot chutes have an internal spiral spring at the base. When the parachute is packed, the spring is compressed. When the ripcord is pulled, the pilot chute springs out, catches air, and produces drag to allow fast, smooth deployment of the main parachute.

Whether your reserve parachute is equipped with a pilot chute depends on the specific emergency procedures you are taught. If you are taught to break away from a malfunctioned main before deploying your reserve, the reserve must be equipped with a pilot chute. If you are taught to deploy your reserve without breakaway (manual deployment), your reserve must not have a pilot chute, because this greatly increases the risk of entangling your reserve and main canopies.

The only type of pilot chute recommended by the USPA is the "spiral/vane" type. There is an older type pilot chute, sometimes found in military reserve parachutes, called the "spider" or "umbrella" type. You should never use this type of pilot chute. It is unsafe because its exposed ribs are easy to snag.

Deployment Device

The deployment device insures an orderly opening sequence

and slows down deployment of the parachute, thus decreasing opening shock. The two most common deployment devices are sleeves and bags. A sleeve is stretched over the parachute canopy much as a shirt sleeve fits over the arm. The parachute canopy is completely stretched out before the sleeve starts to slide off, at which point the canopy begins to catch air and inflate. The bag is more like a pillow case. A bag-deployed canopy is not fully stretched out before inflation begins, but the lines are taut before the canopy is exposed. The deployment device is usually used only with the main parachute; however, some reserves do use a deployment device.

If you have been falling for about 12 seconds, you have reached terminal velocity, the point at which your falling speed is constant. At this speed, your main parachute, which has a deployment device, should open in about 2½ to 3 seconds. Your reserve, by contrast, will open in about 0.7 second.

Canopy

The canopy includes the large "umbrella" under which you descend and the suspension lines, which are sewn to the canopy. The lines are attached to the harness by means of four broad, flat risers made of very strong webbing. All of these parts, and almost all other fabric components, are made of nylon (the deployment device may be made of cotton).

The conventional canopies used by students have diameters of 28, 32, or 35 feet. This diameter is not necessarily a straight-across (open-diameter) measurement; it is usually measured from the lower lateral band (bottom edge) of the canopy, over the apex, and down to the lower lateral band on the opposite side of the canopy (flat diameter).

The heavier beginning jumper should use a larger diameter canopy, since the larger canopies have slower rates of descent. However, diameter is only one of the factors affecting the rate of descent. Many advanced canopies have smaller diameters, but because of the fabric and other design features, they have slower rates of descent.

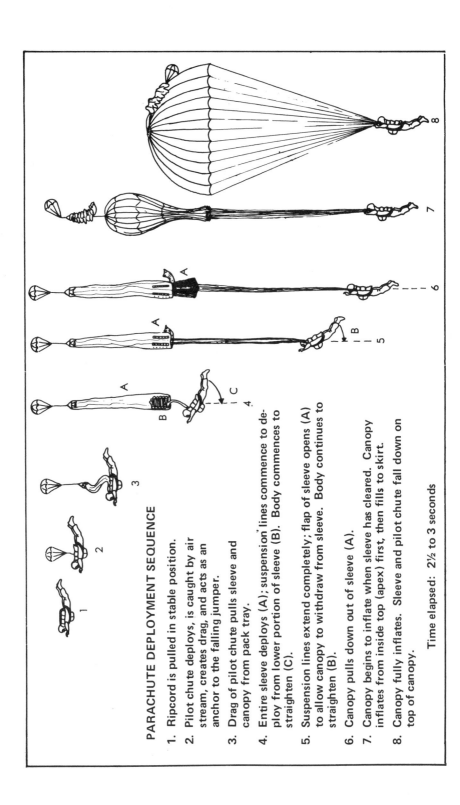

PARACHUTE DEPLOYMENT SEQUENCE

1. Ripcord is pulled in stable position.

2. Pilot chute deploys, is caught by air stream, creates drag, and acts as an anchor to the falling jumper.

3. Drag of pilot chute pulls sleeve and canopy from pack tray.

4. Entire sleeve deploys (A); suspension lines commence to deploy from lower portion of sleeve (B). Body commences to straighten (C).

5. Suspension lines extend completely; flap of sleeve opens (A) to allow canopy to withdraw from sleeve. Body continues to straighten (B).

6. Canopy pulls down out of sleeve (A).

7. Canopy begins to inflate when sleeve has cleared. Canopy inflates from inside top (apex) first, then fills to skirt.

8. Canopy fully inflates. Sleeve and pilot chute fall down on top of canopy.

Time elapsed: 2½ to 3 seconds

Ripcord

The ripcord is the cable, usually made of seven groups of seven-strand steel wires, that pulls the pins out of the cones, allowing the pack to open. The other end of the cable (which is located inside a flexible metal housing to guide it around the curve of the shoulder) is attached to a ripcord handle.

The student, on his first few jumps, does not use a ripcord. Instead, his equipment includes a static line, strong nylon webbing attached to the aircraft, which causes the weight of the jumper to open the container, either by pulling pins or by breaking ties of break-cord.

Container

The container is the part of the parachute assembly that holds the canopy, pilot chute, and deployment device after it is

Some containers require a little "muscle" to close. (Photo by Ron Tavalero)

packed. The container and everything in it are called the "pack." The load, during and after opening, is not supported by the container but by the harness.

Harness

The harness is an assembly of nylon webbing straps and associated hardware that attaches the jumper securely to the canopy. In effect, the harness serves as a "swing" that suspends the jumper beneath the open canopy. The parachutist cannot fall out of the harness because he is held in by a chest strap, two leg straps, two broad vertical straps (called the main lift webbing) down the front of the body, and two diagonal straps across the back. The main lift webbing, chest strap, leg straps, and diagonal straps are all adjustable for a comfortable fit. The harness bears the great stress of opening shock and supports the jumper during the descent under the open canopy. All standard harnesses are rated for far greater stress than they will ever receive during opening shock.

Other Equipment

There are other components of parachute equipment, of

Typical harness. Note "D rings" for attachment of front-mounted reserve. (Photo courtesy of Security Parachute Company)

course, but the major expense in acquiring your own equipment is represented by these six major components. All the major components are supplied by a number of manufacturers and in a variety of styles and brand names.

We will look first at the major components and then examine some complete parachute assemblies, or "rigs," as well as some accessory equipment.

PILOT CHUTES

Type MA-1

This pilot chute, which has a 6-inch hard crown and a 30-inch canopy, can be used in either the main or in the reserve parachute assembly. The vanes, which enclose the spring, may be made of solid fabric or marquisette, a mesh fabric that is less durable but allows air to pass through to aid inflation. The pilot chute has a very strong spring. A military surplus pilot chute, it is also produced by commercial manufacturers. The commercially produced MA-1 has a retail price of about $25, while the surplus price is a few dollars less.

Type A-3

The A-3 pilot chute is regarded by some as superior to the MA-1; however, it is not readily available. It cannot be used in most reserve parachute assemblies. The A-3 has a flat crown, 9 inches in diameter, which has been manufactured both with soft fabric and with stiffer, more durable fabric. It has a 36-inch canopy and a wide, conical spring whose operation is very smooth. The wide spring and wide crown reduce the tendency (more common in the MA-1) to flip over when it is released. Despite its reliable performance, the A-3 has been discontinued by the military and is no longer sold by major parachute equipment distributors.

Para-Commander 36-Inch Pilot Chute

This pilot chute, made by the Pioneer Parachute Company,

Inc., is similar to the MA-1, but its canopy is made of low-permeability fabric. It can be used in either the main or the reserve and costs about $32.

Para-Commander 40-Inch Pilot Chute

This model has a 9-inch hard top and a 40-inch canopy whose vanes are made of marquisette. It is designed for use with the Para-Commander main canopy and costs about $35.

The Grabber

This nonporous pilot chute, available in 36- and 40-inch diameters, has no vanes and an unusually long (34-inch) spring. Manufactured by Strong Enterprises, Inc., it has a 9-inch hard top, and the canopy cannot invert. It was designed to produce quick, sure deployments that are otherwise available only with a dual chute system.

DEPLOYMENT DEVICES

The sleeve has long been the most widely used deployment device in sport parachuting. Almost all students use it because that is what is provided, and the knowledge that allows them to make a choice comes only with experience. (A bag might be safer for students who are likely to open with a poor body position because of the reduced likelihood of entanglement with the canopy in this situation.) Probably a majority of experienced jumpers also use sleeves, at least until they acquire certain types of containers that are more compatible with bags.

Certainly the student who has been taught to pack his parachute with painstaking care is likely to experience some qualms at the sight of an advanced jumper stuffing his canopy into a bag. That does not mean that the sleeve is *safer*. Knowledgeable parachutists can have endless arguments on the subject. Both the sleeve and the bag are safe deployment devices, and each has advantages and disadvantages.

Both serve the same purpose: to contain the canopy; to pro-

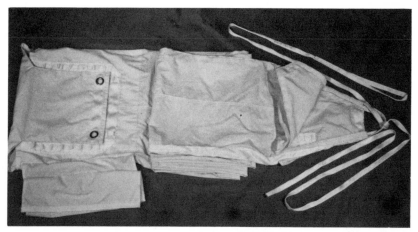

Para-Commander short sleeve, a deployment device. (Photo courtesy of Parachutes Incorporated)

vide an orderly sequence of deployment; and to slow the opening, reducing opening shock. They are similar in construction except for length. The *sleeve* encloses the entire length of the canopy, or at least most of it, while the canopy must be "S-folded" into a *bag*.

With both devices, the suspension lines are stowed on the *outside*, and the deployment device is kept closed by means of a flap and two "locking" stows of the lines until full line stretch is achieved during the opening sequence. Only then does the deployment device let the canopy out.

Some jumpers prefer a sleeve because less drag is required to lift it out of the container. However, there is more than enough drag produced by any standard pilot chute to lift the entire weight of a bag and canopy, although it may not lift as readily at low air speeds. The greatest advantage of the bag is that it has much less bulk than the sleeve, and the container can be closed more easily than with a sleeve.

Both sleeves and bags are made in a great variety of styles, sizes, and construction. The price of a sleeve ranges from about $35 to about $60; that of a bag, somewhere toward the lower end of that range.

A much newer type of deployment device is the "POD," or Para-Opener Device, developed by Parachutes Incorporated. The canopy is placed in it much as if it were being packed into a reserve container, producing a compact, neat pack easily accepted by the main container. This device is used with high performance canopies that have apex crown lines.

CANOPIES

Conventional Main Parachute Canopies

Almost all students start jumping with conventional canopies, which are military surplus canopies modified for sport parachuting use. Most of these canopies have a diameter of 28 feet, although 32- and 35-foot canopies are also in use. In general, the 35-foot canopies are reserved for heavier students, since these canopies have a slower rate of descent, and weight is an important factor in the force of landing.

In some experimental programs, students are permitted to start jumping on the Para-Commander (PC), a parachute normally used only by more experienced jumpers, but most students must jump conventional canopies. The PC has a much slower rate of descent, allowing soft landings, but in the hands of an inexperienced jumper, it can be accidentally stalled, producing a much faster rate of descent and the possibility of serious injury. In addition, its greater forward speed increases the chance of injury on a downwind landing. Thus, students have to accept the harder landings of conventional canopies, and they prepare for them by drill in parachute landing falls (PLFs).

A conventional canopy with a slower rate of descent is the "Lopo" (for "low-porosity"), which can be purchased new from commercial manufacturers. Since these canopies cost quite a bit more than the surplus conventional canopies, their introduction led to the nickname "cheapo" for the high-porosity canopies.

Conventional round canopy with modifications for steering. (USPA photo)

Porosity is the key factor (but not the only one) in deter-mining the rate of descent of a canopy. Cheapos are usually constructed of 1.1 fabric, while Lopos are usually made of 1.6. The designations refer to the weight in ounces of one square yard of fabric. The fabric of the Lopo has its permeability re-duced by a process involving heat and pressure, called calen-dering, which flattens and spreads the fibers so that there is less space between them.

Porosity is directly related to permeability, which is mea-sured in terms of the flow of air through the fabric of an open canopy, including the holes, during its descent. The permea-bility of the cheapo is 100 to 160 cubic feet per minute (cfm) through one square foot of fabric. The Lopo, by comparison, has a permeability of 80 to 120 cfm, and the PC, which is made largely of 2.2 taffeta, has almost no permeability—0 to 10 cfm.

Conventional canopies are usually "modified" to produce forward speed and steerability. "Modification" refers to the fabric cut out of the canopy, producing holes through which air rushes out to produce thrust, or forward speed. The modifi-cations are of different patterns, each of which produces a specific type of performance and varying thrust.

The forward speed of a conventional canopy is widely vari-able, depending on its size, construction, material, design, type of modification, and the weight of the jumper. No one seems to know for sure just what the various forward speeds are, but the forward speed of a conventional canopy probably varies from around 3 mph to perhaps 12 mph, with the average forward speed in the range of 6 to 8 mph.

The modification is a "window" cut into the canopy. The most common modifications are the Double L, 5-panel TU, and 7-panel TU, although many others are occasionally seen. Modification produces thrust, which gives the canopy forward speed and also allows it to be steered. Steering lines go up to the vent modifications. If you want to turn right, you pull down on the right-hand steering line. This distorts the right-hand modification, deflecting the flow of air toward the front of the canopy on that side. Since there is now more thrust to the rear on the left-hand side, the canopy is pushed around to the right. If both steering lines are pulled down, the deflection of air toward the front of the canopy results in *braking*. This deflection principle is the reason a 7-panel TU has better braking than a canopy with a 3- or 5-panel separation between open gores.

Steerability is an obvious advantage, since the parachutist can control his flight over the ground, avoid obstacles, and achieve a high degree of accuracy in landing.

The student is not much concerned with precision accuracy; that comes later, with more experience and higher performance parachutes. For the student, steerability means he can find a safe place to land, and he can cancel out most or all of his speed over the ground (by facing into the wind) for an easier landing.

Modified cheapos cost upwards of $100, depending on the diameter and type of modification. Unmodified canopies cost about $20 less, but you will have to pay that to have it modified anyway, so you might as well buy a modified canopy in the first place.

A 28-foot Pioneer low-porosity canopy, with factory modification and a wide variety of colorful designs, costs around $400.

If you are buying your first parachute, you are probably not interested in the price of a canopy alone. A complete surplus rig (main and reserve parachute assemblies, including harness and conventional main canopy) can be purchased for around $200 from major distributors. If you shop around among jumpers, you can sometimes buy a complete rig for less, since people often sell their cheapo (conventional) rigs when they move on to higher performance equipment. If you buy a rig from an individual, be sure you have a rigger or some other experienced parachutist check it out to be sure it is in good condition and safe for jumping.

Sport parachutes are divided into four general categories:

conventional canopies (already described), high-performance canopies, wing-type canopies, and ram-air canopies. (The last two categories have even higher performance, are quite expensive, and are usually used only by very experienced jumpers.)

High-Performance Canopies

All canopies in this category are round except for the Thunderbow, which is triangular, but they look quite different from conventional canopies. They have more vents and other features are different. Though identified as "high-performance," this term is a little misleading, because they are not the highest-performance canopies. Here are the high-performance canopies in general use in the United States.

Mark I Para-Commander (PC). First marketed (and first used by the U.S. Team) in 1964, the Mark I PC had a revolutionary effect on accuracy competition, and it is by far the most widely used canopy, among experienced jumpers, in the United States. Like most other high-performance canopies, it has sta-

Mark I Para-commander from the jumper's point of view. (Photo by Andy Keech)

bilizer panels below the canopy proper and a pulled-down apex, which produces more desirable aerodynamic characteristics. It has a maximum forward speed of about 14 mph, and it can be braked to shut off almost all forward speed. Even more braking (pulling down the steering lines) produces a stall that, while it can be dangerous near the ground, is useful for achieving a rapid loss of altitude when necessary (for example, when you want to increase vertical separation from another jumper). In a stall, the PC (and similar canopies) has a rate of descent of 30 feet per second (fps) or more. Its normal rate of descent is about 14 to 16 fps, compared with about 18 fps for a 28-foot cheapo. It costs around $400.

Mark II Para-Commander. This simplified version of the Mark I was introduced in 1969. It was supposed to have somewhat better stability (and a little less drive) than the Mark I, but the enthusiasm for the new design rapidly wore off, and few jumpers now use the Mark II. Some of the improvements that the Mark II was supposed to achieve can be made by modifying the Mark I.

Competition Para-Commander. This improved design of the Mark I has reduced the length of the suspension lines by 42 inches. It has larger steering slots and heavy duty crown lines, as well as certain other design changes. When used by an experienced parachutist, it can be an excellent accuracy canopy. It costs around $400.

Russian Para-Commander. Like other Para-Commanders, this canopy is made by Pioneer. It is very similar to the Russian UT-15, with which the Russian team won the gold medal in team accuracy in the 1972 World Parachuting Championships. The Pioneer copy is marketed in both 23- and 27-foot diameters.

U.S. Papillon. Made by Paraflite, Inc., this is a somewhat improved, better-constructed version of the French Papillon. Its chief design feature is a smoother, more stable "sink" throughout the low-speed range, which is important for accuracy. It costs around $400.

Thunderbow. This is a triangular parachute made by Security Parachute Company. Despite its initial billing, this is not a good accuracy canopy, partly because of the sluggishness of its turns. Its forward speed is roughly comparable to that of a Para-Commander, and it has very reliable openings. Its low malfunction rate makes it a good canopy for all applications except accuracy. It costs under $400.

Crossbow. The Crossbow, introduced in 1964, is rarely seen, because it was eclipsed by the Para-Commander, which is more stable and capable of better accuracy. Its drive is comparable to that of the Para-Commander.

Wing-Type Canopies

Delta II Para-Wing. First manufactured by Irving Industries, Inc. and then developed and marketed in 1968 by Steve Snyder, the Delta II Para-Wing is the only wing-type canopy in general use in the United States. As the name implies, it has a "delta" shape. Its chief attraction is novelty; it is not a good accuracy canopy. It can glide about twice as far as a Para-Commander. A good many parachutists who failed to recognize the radical differences in handling this canopy have suffered serious injuries. Nevertheless, when flown by someone who takes the trouble to learn its particular flying characteristics, it is no more of a problem than the canopies I have defined as "high-performance." It is no longer generally available, although many are found among sport parachutists. It is included in this chapter because it is the only successful delta design that has been marketed in the United States. If you can find a new one, it will cost you under $400.

Ram-Air Canopies

The ram-air canopies are a truly revolutionary development in parachutes. Rectangular in shape and with forward speeds greatly exceeding those of the best high-performance canopies, they have flying characteristics that make them much more similar to gliders than to conventional parachutes, in-

Delta II Para-Wing. (Photo by Jerry Irwin)

cluding the high-performance conventional canopies. They are capable of very shallow glide angles, but they can be spiraled, losing altitude with startling speed. And they are capable of slow, feather-soft landings and other flight characteristics that make them formidable accuracy canopies.

The principle of the Ram-Air Multicell Airfoil was conceived in 1963 by Domina Jalbert, but serious technical problems had to be solved before a ram-air canopy for sport parachutists could be marketed.

Steve Snyder, founder of Paraflite, Inc., advanced the basic ram-air concept by developing the first "man-rated" ram-air canopy produced for sport parachutists.

The ram-air canopy has a high lift/drag (glide) ratio compared to other canopy designs, producing a much more shallow glide angle. The ram-air can achieve about three times the glide of a Para-Commander or about 50 percent more glide than the Delta II Para-Wing. A jumper, descending under his canopy from one mile above the ground and with no wind, would be able to travel about three miles over the ground with a ram-air canopy, about two miles with a Delta II Para-Wing, and a little over one mile with a Para-Commander.

Seven ram-air canopies have been manufactured in the United States, of which two, the Volplane (Pioneer) and the Para-Foil (Paraflite, Inc.), are no longer distributed. All five ram-air canopies described in this section cost about the same: around $600, including the deployment device.

Para-Plane. This canopy, manufactured by Paraflite, Inc., is often called the standard or "small" Para-Plane to distinguish it from a later design called the Cloud. Its maximum forward speed is about 25 to 28 mph, which is somewhat greater than that of the more recently developed Cloud. Users of all ram-air canopies should thoroughly read and understand the specific instruction manual for each, but this advice is especially urged for users of the small Para-Plane because of its very rapid response. A jumper's error in judgment coupled with slowness in response to a changing flight situation can result in serious injury.

Para-Plane Cloud. Also produced by Paraflite, Inc., the Cloud is probably the most popular of the ram-air canopies. The Cloud has less forward speed than the small Para-Plane (its maximum is about 20 to 22 mph). It also has better "slow flight" characteristics than either the small Para-Plane or the Para-Sled. Few knowledgeable jumpers would argue with the statement that the Cloud is the best of the ram-airs for accuracy.

Para-Sled. The manufacturer of the Para-Sled, Aero Foil Systems, Inc., has gone out of business, but the Para-Sled will continue to be distributed until present stocks are exhausted.

Designer Steve Snyder under the small Para-Plane. (Photo by Gary Patmor)

New Strato-Star ram-air canopy. (Photo courtesy of Steve Snyder Enterprises, Inc.)

The Para-Sled is comparable to the small Para-Plane in forward speed, but it requires less toggle pressure for steering and braking, and it is more compact when packed than the Cloud. Current competition results indicate that the Para-Sled is inferior to the Cloud in accuracy.

Jalbert Para-Foil. The Jalbert patents, under which the Para-Sled was formerly manufactured, have been assigned to North American Dynamics, Inc. Prototypes of a new ram-air canopy, to be manufactured by that company, are now being tested and will be on the market in 1975. Since the design is not "frozen," specific information is not available, but the Jalbert Para-Foil is intended as a precision accuracy ram-air canopy.

Strato-Star. A new ram-air canopy, the Strato-Star, has now

The Beechnuts, a 10-man team in competition at the 1974 U.S. Nationals, jump the new Strato-Star ram-air canopy in its specially designed container. (Photo by Jerry Irwin)

been extensively tested and is now available from the manufacturer, Paraflite, Inc. The Strato-Star was designed with the relative worker in mind. Aerodynamically, it behaves and inflates very much like a conventional round canopy. Of great importance to relative workers is the fact that the new canopy has very little "surge" on opening. The design of the deployment system yields low opening shock and symmetrical openings with little of the "twist" associated with other ram-air canopies. The manufacturer reports that the glide performance is about the same as that of the Cloud, but the Strato-Star has 25 percent less area and 40 percent less bulk. Its small size, also of importance to relative workers, means that it cannot be safely fitted into a standard container. Thus, it is marketed with a special container that is, in effect, part of the entire parachute deployment system. It costs about $500.

RESERVE CANOPIES

The sport parachutist is required, both by law and by common sense, to jump with two parachutes: a main and an auxiliary (reserve). While the sport parachutist normally packs his own main, the reserve must be inspected and repacked by an FAA-certificated rigger within 60 days of any jump. (This repack cycle goes back to the days of silk parachutes, when it was reasonable. A change to a repack cycle of 120 days is under consideration by the FAA and will probably be a reality in the near future.)

Reserves are available in a wide range of designs and prices.

Strong 26-foot low-porosity reserve. (Photo courtesy of Strong Enterprises, Inc.)

Both surplus and commercially manufactured canopies are used by jumpers, but some of the surplus canopies are becoming very scarce.

Surplus Canopies

These canopies are available in diameters of 24, 26, and 28 feet. The 28-foot canopy, equipped with a deployment device, is also a main.

If you are considering the purchase of a 24-foot reserve canopy, be careful. This canopy is made from two different types of fabric, twill and ripstop. The twill canopy will save your life, but anything else is gravy. If you have a 24-foot twill, use it for a car cover and get yourself a good reserve for jumping. The 24-foot ripstop, when properly modified for steering, is a stable, slow-descending, rugged canopy that will provide a landing that is not noticeably harder than that experienced on the 28-foot reserve.

Most students, and a good many advanced jumpers, use 28-foot surplus canopies. They are safe, and they are far less expensive than the commercial canopies.

The 26-foot Navy conical is a very good surplus canopy, but it is very hard to find, and the inevitable result is that the price is climbing rapidly. Many experienced jumpers do jump the 26-foot Navy conical and regard it as a perfectly satisfactory reserve.

Commercial Canopies

These canopies are far more expensive than the surplus canopies—they start at over $200—but your reserve is your *last* canopy. For your own peace of mind, you will probably want to spend the money. The commercial reserves have good drive and maneuverability, and their low-porosity construction means that your landing will usually be softer than it would be under a surplus reserve.

The choice of a commercial reserve is largely a matter of money and personal taste. While a number of them are presently on the market, detailed descriptions would not be very useful to you. You can learn more by talking to experienced parachutists.

HARNESSES AND CONTAINERS

Harnesses and containers may be purchased separately and then assembled, but few parachutists do this. The harness and main container are usually bought as a unit. Many commercially manufactured assemblies can be purchased with the harness and both main and reserve containers in matching colors.

If you do buy your reserve container separately, you should note that designs are widely variable. The hardware on some reserve canopies is not compatible with that on your main harness. Some changes may have to be made in either type or position. Otherwise, the reserve may be slung awkwardly low, or it may be mounted so high that it covers your main ripcord handle. Be sure all your equipment is compatible.

Surplus Harness and Containers

As a student, you will probably use surplus equipment. (In fact, many experienced jumpers do.) It is less expensive than commercially available equipment, and it is not as pretty; but it is entirely safe. At least it is safe as manufactured. Any time you buy used equipment, surplus or commercial, you should be sure it is inspected by an FAA-certificated rigger.

You can buy a surplus harness with both main and reserve containers for under $50, but you will probably pay considerably more. Major distributors of parachute equipment sell both surplus and commercial assemblies.

Commercial Harnesses and Containers

The "standard" commercial assemblies, manufactured by parachute equipment companies such as Pioneer, Security, North American Aerodynamics, and Strong Enterprises, come in a wide variety of colors and designs. The reserve container is compatible with the main (although it may be purchased

Greene Star tandem (piggyback) main and reserve parachutes. (Photo courtesy of Greene Star Systems)

separately). Most of these assemblies have a front-mounted reserve, but some manufacturers also produce tandem, or "piggyback," versions.

The piggyback rig has a back-mounted reserve which is located on top of the main. It is generally more comfortable and allows greater freedom of movement in the airplane, an important consideration for the Jumpmaster who must deal with students in a crowded airplane. Many jumpers prefer the piggyback for relative work. An important disadvantage of the piggyback system is that the reserve is out of sight *behind* you. You *must* break away from a malfunctioned main, and this presents an uncomfortable (and dangerous) situation if the reserve, because of a "pack closure" or pilot chute hesitation, does not open immediately.

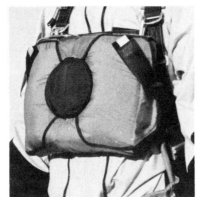

POP TOP reserve. (Photo courtesy of Strong Enterprises, Inc.)

Fastback main container with POP TOP reserve. (Photo courtesy of Strong Enterprises, Inc.)

You must use the breakaway for reserve deployment in case of a partial malfunction if you use a piggyback, because with both parachutes located on your back, there is great danger of entanglement if you manually deploy your reserve without breakaway.

Since commercial harnesses and containers come in a wide variety of designs, it is understandable that the price is also widely variable. Commercial harness and container assemblies, including both containers, start at around $200 and range upward to about $350 or $400.

Custom Harness and Containers

There has been a trend, during the last few years, toward

custom equipment that caters to the customer's individual taste by providing a wider choice of color and other design specifications. Custom rigs, most of which are produced by small manufacturers, are widely variable in price.

A note of caution about custom equipment is in order. While some designs are entirely safe, others have not been sufficiently tested before marketing and are subject to pack closures and other deficiencies. Before you rush out and buy a beautiful (and expensive) custom rig, try to get as much information as possible from experienced jumpers who own the brand you are interested in. The owner of a custom rig may be able to tell you things you could never learn from the manufacturer. I am not suggesting that you do not buy custom rigs; I *am* suggesting that you be careful.

POP TOP Reserve

While innovations in reserves have been introduced in sport parachuting over the last several years (center-pull ripcord for a less exposed position; swivel cones to reduce the chance of pin locks), one revolutionary reserve design is worth special mention. The POP TOP reserve, by Strong Enterprises, Inc., was developed to fill the needs of large-star relative workers, whose fast mass exits from the airplane are sometimes impeded by the jamming of a conventional reserve against other jumpers or the door. And there is always the possibility of snagging a reserve handle, which is a very dangerous situation. Even if the jumper is not hurt by the premature opening of his parachute, he is left helplessly hanging under his reserve canopy, thousands of feet above the building star.

The POP TOP reserve is only 2 inches thick. The pilot chute is compressed *outside* the reserve container, and the ripcord handle is located at the back of the container, where it is completely protected. The container wraps around the body for a clean profile, important for good freefall maneuvering, and the whole assembly weighs under 10 pounds. The POP TOP reserve costs about $80 for the container, cap, and ripcord.

ACCESSORY EQUIPMENT

You need several items of accessory equipment for sport parachuting, including boots, helmet, jumpsuit, altimeter, gloves, goggles, stopwatches, and automatic openers.

Boots

Since the landing force can be pretty hard on unsupported ankles, boots are a standard item of parachuting equipment. Students have to wear adequate boots, and most jumpers use them. (Some experienced jumpers wear sneakers, moccasins, or other footwear that gives no support, but by the time you reach that level of experience, you can make up your own mind.)

By far the most widely used boots among sport parachutists are the Paraboots, which are imported from France and cost about $50. These boots have well-cushioned pneumatic soles with locked-in air pockets and are quite comfortable. A lighter weight, less heavily reinforced model of the Paraboot is available for style jumpers for a little less.

However, other boots, such as Army airborne (paratrooper) boots, are adequate. The main consideration is that they extend above the ankles and give them support. If you use boots with lacing hooks, be sure the hooks are covered with tape before you jump. If you should open in a bad body position, you could snag suspension lines or pilot chute on the boots.

Helmet

The Basic Safety Regulations of the USPA require the use of a rigid or HALO helmet. (The HALO helmet, developed for the Army's High Altitude, Low Opening project, is a soft helmet with a network of rigid ribs for protection.) A good helmet is necessary to avoid injury from midair collisions and hard landings. It is also good protection during the parachute opening, when risers and connector links lift past the head. If a student (or advanced jumper) is unstable at pull time, the hardware could strike the unprotected head. And the jumper who bangs his head in the aircraft is grateful for his helmet.

Most jumpers use some version of the Bell helmet, which costs between $40 and $50, but you should avoid the models with visors or face shields, because these can be blown off in freefall.

The American National Standards Institute has established the Z90.1 standards for protective helmets, and the Safety Helmet Council of America (SHCA) independently tests helmets. You should look for either a Z90.1 or an SHCA sticker inside the helmet.

Jumpsuit

The jumpsuit is a protective coverall that gives warmth during the ride up and the jump, and it keeps your clothing clean and your body free of scrapes and cuts during landings. It also produces drag to improve your maneuverability during freefall.

Many innovations have been introduced during the last few years because of the rapid growth of relative work. Some jumpsuits have extra material under the arms for additional lift, and they may have bells on the arms, legs, or both. These design elements help the heavier jumper to "float," brake more quickly, or otherwise improve freefall maneuvering.

Many commercial and custom designs are on the market. They range in price from about $40 to about $80 or $90. However, the student who wants to keep his initial expenses low will find the ordinary workman's coveralls are quite adequate and far less expensive; at least until he decides he wants to stay with sport parachuting.

Gloves

The Basic Safety Regulations require the use of gloves if the air temperature is under 40° F. Most jumpers use gloves on all jumps, because they give protection on landing and aid in freefall maneuvering. Almost any well-fitting glove is suitable, but it should not be so bulky that it interferes with your ability to break away from a malfunction or to grasp the ripcord handle. No bare skin should be exposed below the jumpsuit cuff.

Goggles

A wide variety of goggles are commercially available. Your goggles should be chosen with both safety and comfort in mind. Some types of large goggles with heavy rubber seals around the edges should not be used, because they interfere with peripheral vision and sometimes make it difficult to see the ripcord handle. And some of the larger goggles can blow off in freefall.

The smallest goggles available, the Portia, are also the cheapest. They cost about a dollar, but they break quickly. They are very shallow and fit closely around the eyes, but some jumpers find them uncomfortable because of the sharp edges.

You can see in freefall without goggles, but the atmosphere is filled with tiny particles that irritate the eyes and can cause problems after a while. And when you have to stick your head out into the air stream to spot, you quickly learn to appreciate goggles. Some people experience watering of the eyes, which interferes with vision.

Some goggles are available with either clear or amber lenses. But amber lenses do reduce depth perception somewhat; and of course they should not be used on night jumps or late in the day.

If you wear glasses, you don't need goggles; but you should be sure to secure the glasses with an eyeglass strap.

Altimeters

The USPA recommends the use of an altimeter or a stopwatch (or both) for freefalls of more than 20 seconds. (On short delays, you can keep track of the time by counting.) The alti-

The Altimaster II altimeter. (photo courtesy of Steve Snyder Enterprises, Inc.)

meter is also useful in planning accuracy approaches to the target.

The two altimeters most widely used by sport parachutists are the Altimaster II, by Steve Snyder Enterprises, and the North Star, by North American Aerodynamics. Each costs about $50, and each has the area from 2,500 feet down to zero clearly marked in red.

Each of these altimeters may be mounted on a panel, which also accepts a stopwatch, for use on the chest-mounted reserve, or it may be used with a wrist mount. Students are usually discouraged from using the wrist mount until they can maneuver well in freefall.

A less expensive altimeter, designed for use on the reserve, is the Aero Indicator. This altimeter has a Kollsman window like that on aircraft altimeters and phosphorescent markings for use on night jumps.

A French-made altimeter, the Para-Control Wrist Altimeter, is now available in the United States. It costs about $65.

Stopwatches

Many sport parachutists use a stopwatch instead of—or in addition to—an altimeter, and thus keep track of time instead of altitude. But if you don't remember to start the watch when

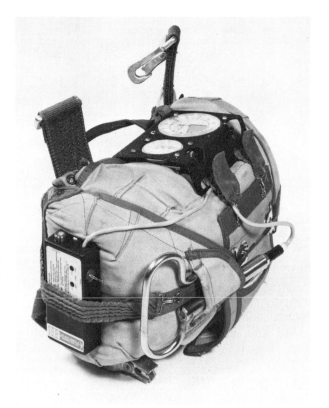

Sentinel MK 2000 automatic opener mounted on reserve. (Photo courtesy of Steve Snyder Enterprises, Inc.)

you leave the airplane, it is useless. The price of a good stop-watch ranges from about $25 to about $50. Like the altimeter, it may be worn either on the reserve or on the wrist.

Automatic Openers

The USPA recommends the use of an automatic opening device as a backup system for *all* parachute jumps. This is a device that automatically opens a parachute if the jumper fails to do so. The device is calibrated for activation at around 1,000 to 1,400 feet, which is well below the normal opening altitude.

At present, the Basic Safety Regulations do not require the automatic opener, even for students; and thus the advice, which is not binding on USPA members, is largely ignored by advanced jumpers. Worse, a great many clubs and commercial centers do not even require *students* to use an automatic opener.

I have no quarrel with experienced jumpers who choose not to use an automatic opener, unless some physical condition, such as epilepsy, presents the possibility that the jumper may lose consciousness during freefall. However, I have some very strong opinions where *students* are concerned.

Of the 44 fatalities in the United States in 1973 (an unusually bad year), 15 were *students* with 25 or fewer jumps, and 5 of these died on the first jump. Of the 15, 10 either failed to pull either ripcord or failed to open the reserve after a total malfunction of the main parachute. These statistics should make obvious the necessity for an automatic opener on student jumps, or at least on the early jumps.

Automatic openers are expensive, but in view of the statistics, this should not be a consideration. I believe an early-jump student should not be denied the safety of an automatic opener. If you are planning to start sport parachuting, I strongly urge you to get your training with a club or center that *requires* automatic openers for students on the first several jumps.

Of the three automatic openers currently available in the United States, two may be used either with the reserve or the main parachute, and only one, the Sentinel MK 2000, is primarily designed for use with the reserve. I believe the automatic opener should be used with the *reserve* parachute. It will *not* open a main parachute in case of a total malfunction of the main and is therefore useless in that situation.

The *Sentinel MK 2000* automatic opener, manufactured by Steve Snyder Enterprises, is probably the safest and most reliable device currently available. At around $150, it is also the least expensive. The simple calibration procedure, necessary before each jump, also checks out the electrical circuitry, the battery, and the firing cartridge.

A forerunner of the Sentinel MK 2000 had to be turned off manually after the main parachute opened. It also had to be armed after the aircraft was well above the calibrated firing altitude. The new design operates on both barometric pressure and *rate of descent*. It turns itself on and off and fires only when it is needed. Thus, the parachutist merely calibrates the device on the ground and then forgets it, with one exception: It must be deactivated if the jump is aborted and the airplane makes a rapid descent.

The *FXC Model 8000*, manufactured by the FXC Corporation and the newest automatic opening device on the market, also incorporates the rate of descent feature. It has no electrical circuitry, and the activating device is a spring-operated cable rather than an explosive squib. This device, formerly made by the HI-TEK Corporation, had a problem in the field that was traced to a heat-treated spring, but the new manufacturer reports that all affected units were recalled and the problem was corrected. The Model 8000 costs about $250.

The *KAP-3*, manufactured in Czechoslovakia and the Soviet Union and marketed by some American distributors, is advertised as compatible with either the main or reserve, but it is designed for use with the main. It incorporates both an aneroid pressure-sensing device and a clockwork timing mechanism. The actuation device is mechanical. The KAP-3 is extremely simple, rugged, and reliable. It costs a little over $200.

Appendix A
The Organization of Sport Parachuting

The only official national organization of sport parachutists in the United States is the United States Parachute Association (USPA), a nonprofit division of the National Aeronautic Association. It is the official representative of the Federation Aeronautique Internationale (FAI) for parachuting in the United States, and it is the national representative body for parachutists, parachute riggers, and the parachute industry. It is the only national organization sanctioning sport parachuting competition in the United States.

WHAT THE USPA DOES

As the national organization of sport parachuting, the USPA:

- promotes safety in parachuting and establishes safety standards and recommended procedures for safe jumping
- promotes and sanctions competitive sport parachuting and establishes standards for competition
- supervises and officially documents all parachuting record attempts in the United States
- encourages unity among all persons interested in parachuting
- encourages the study and knowledge of parachuting among the membership and the general public
- compiles and publishes monthly information about the sport and technology of parachuting through its official publication, *Parachutist* magazine, and other publications

- cooperates with all governmental agencies dealing with aeronautics to promote the public safety
- selects and trains the United States Parachute Team for international competition
- fosters and encourages (through its affiliate, the National Collegiate Parachuting League) the development of parachuting as an intercollegiate sport
- cooperates with other sporting aviation groups in the preservation and promotion of sporting and general aviation activities in the United States

The most visible benefit of membership in the USPA is the monthly magazine *Parachutist*, but there are other important advantages. It offers its membership, currently numbering about 20,000:

- insurance protection—$10,000/$20,000 public liability and $5,000 property damage (its current insurance carrier is Lloyd's of London)
- eligibility for competition in USPA-sanctioned meets
- eligibility for participation in national and international record attempts
- eligibility for international parachuting licenses
- representation before local, state, and federal government
- a voice in the government and operation of the USPA
- USPA insignia and credentials
- guidance and assistance in all sport parachuting activities

Safety

While safety is the concern of every sport parachutist, the general monitoring of safety is the responsibility of area safety officers and club safety officers.

The area safety officer (ASO) is responsible for the conduct of safe parachuting operations in a particular geographical area, usually including several clubs or drop zones. The ASO is recommended for appointment by his conference director. He may certify all parachuting licenses and approves night, water, and exhibition jumps. He may certify annual validation requirements for the Jumpmaster rating. If he holds the Instructor rating, he may certify the renewal of this rating as well.

The club safety officer (CSO) is appointed by the ASO, who decides the number of CSO's necessary for the monitoring of safety at individual clubs or drop zones. The CSO may certify the Class A license only.

Licenses

The USPA issues four classes of parachuting licenses recognized by all member nations of the Federation Aeronautique Internationale:

- Class A. At least 25 freefall parachute jumps and certain other proficiency requirements. The holder of a Class A license may jump without supervision and is eligible for competition.
- Class B. At least 50 freefalls and other proficiency requirements. The holder of a Class B license may participate in relative work, make record attempts, and is eligible for appointment as a CSO.
- Class C. At least 100 freefalls and other proficiency requirements. The holder of the Class C license may take part in night, water, and exhibition jumps. (Some states, such as California, require the D license for exhibition jumps.) The C-licensed parachutist is eligible for appointment as an ASO and for the Jumpmaster and Instructor ratings.
- Class D. At least 200 freefalls and other proficiency requirements. The holder of the D license is regarded as an expert parachutist and is eligible for the Instructor/Examiner rating, which is the elite rating of sport parachuting.

Ratings

Competence in the instruction and supervision of students and (when required) other parachutists is assured by a system of three ratings. Starting with the lowest in rank, these are:

- Jumpmaster. Holds a C or D license. May jumpmaster static line and freefall students. Has passed both theoretical and practical examinations administered by an Instructor/Examiner or by an ASO who holds an Instructor rating.
- Instructor. Holds all privileges of the Jumpmaster rating and must hold a C or D license for eligibility. USPA Basic Safety Regulations require that the training of first-jump students must be under the supervision of an Instructor. He may also give advanced instruction and certify Class A licenses. He may administer the *written examination* for any license which he holds.
- Instructor/Examiner. Holds all privileges of the Jumpmaster and Instructor ratings. As an expert in all phases of parachuting, he must hold the D license and be an FAA-certificated rigger. He must pass extensive written and practical examinations. He may certify all classes of parachuting licenses and ratings. He may supervise night, water, and exhibition jumps.

Awards

A number of achievements in sport parachuting are recognized by the USPA through a system of awards. These are:

- USPA Achievement Award. This is the highest award in American sport parachuting and has been presented only three times in the history of the organization. It is presented only for major contributions in any area of sport parachuting.
- Gold Expert Parachutist Badge. The "Gold Wings" are presented to a USPA member who is a U.S. citizen,

holds the D license, and has made 1,000 parachute jumps under the provisions of the Basic Safety Regulations.

- Gold Expert Parachutist Badge with Diamond(s). Same requirements as for the Gold Wings, except that the Diamond Wings recognize 2,000 freefalls and the Double Diamond Wings recognize 3,000 freefalls.
- Gold Freefall Badge. Awarded to a USPA member who is a U.S. citizen, holds the D license, and has logged 12 hours of freefall time.
- Diamond Freefall Badge. Same requirements as for the Gold Freefall Badge except that the award recognizes 24 hours of freefall time.

The mail address of USPA Headquarters is P.O. Box 109, Monterey, California 93940. The telephone number is (408) 373-2708.

THE INTERNATIONAL ORGANIZATION

Almost all nations in which there is significant sport parachuting or other aviation sport activity are members of the Federation Aeronautique Internationale (International Aeronautic Federation). Delegates from member nations meet annually at FAI Headquarters in Paris.

Of particular interest to sport parachutists is a division called the International Parachuting Committee (CIP). While the FAI was founded in 1905, the CIP did not come into existence until 1950.

The FAI, through the CIP, sanctions all international parachuting competitions, establishes the rules for such competitions, and regulates and certifies all world record attempts.

Appendix B
Summary of the World
Championships

The World Parachuting Championships, sanctioned by the Federation Aeronautique International (FAI), were first held in St. Yan, France, in 1951 and became a biennial event in 1954, when the second world meet was held in Bratislava, Czechoslovakia. Now held in each even-numbered year, the Twelfth World Parachuting Championships took place in Szolnok, Hungary, in 1974. The World Parachuting Championships include style and accuracy as individual events and team accuracy.

Relative work has now come into its own, and the first World Parachuting Championships of Relative Work will be held in West Germany in 1975 and will also be a biennial event in odd-numbered years.

The following summary of World Parachuting Championships is based on information provided by the International Parachuting Committee (CIP) of the FAI and from USPA files. Some first names of competitors were not available, and the spellings of many Eastern European names differ from conventional English, since the original information was provided in French.

I. Bled, Yugoslavia, 1951

Six nations were represented; 15 men and 2 women competed. Pierre Lard, of France, was named World Champion, followed in the standings by Vojo Vukcevic, Yugoslavia, and Hans Walti, Switzerland. The two women were Monique LaRoche, France, placing ahead of Valentina Seliverstova, Soviet Union. The United States was not represented.

II. Saint Yan, France, 1954

There were 31 competitors, including the same two women (who reversed their standings at this return match). The men's standings were Ivan Fedchichine, U.S.S.R., first; Vasilij Marjutkin, U.S.S.R., second; and Sam Chasak, France, third. The national standings were: U.S.S.R., first; Czechoslovakia, second; and France, third. The lone American representative was Fred Mason, then in the Army and stationed in Germany. This meet established the pattern of World Parachuting Championships held each even-numbered year, which has continued ever since.

III. Moscow, U.S.S.R., 1956

The 73 competitors included 23 women, and the United States was represented by a full men's team but no women's team. This first U.S. Team included George Bosworth, Walter Fair, Floyd Hobby, Lyle Hoffman, Jacques Istel, Lew Sanborn, and George Stone. The men's standings were Kubek, Ozabel, and Jehlicka, all of Czechoslovakia. Josefa Maxova, Czechoslovakia, placed first in the women's division, followed by Seliverstova and Mouchina of U.S.S.R. The men's team standings were: Czechoslovakia, first; U.S.S.R., second; and Bulgaria, third. (The U.S. placed sixth of the 10 nations competing.) The women's team standings were: U.S.S.R., first; Czechoslovakia, second; and Bulgaria, third.

IV. Bratislava, Czechoslovakia, 1958

Fourteen nations fielded 78 competitors, including 21 women. In the men's division, Pjotr Ostrovski, U.S.S.R., took first place; Jehlicka, Czechoslovakia, was second; and Milicevic, Yugoslavia, finished third. Of the women, the top three places went to Nadja Prischinova, U.S.S.R.; Franksova, Poland; and Valceva, Bulgaria. The men's team standings were U.S.S.R., first; Czechoslovakia, second; and Bulgaria, third. The women's team standings were U.S.S.R., first; Poland, second; and Bulgaria, third.

V. Sofia, Bulgaria, 1960

The 137 competitors from 12 nations included 42 women. Jim Arender became World Style Champion, and Dick Fortenberry took second place overall in the men's division. This was the first time Americans had broken into the winning column. Standings of the men were Zdenek Kaplan, Czechoslovakia, who also won the world accuracy championship; Dick Fortenberry, U.S.A., second; and Anikejev, U.S.S.R., third. The women's standings were Bozena Rejzlova, Czechoslovakia, first; Zoubova, U.S.S.R., second; and Rybova, Czechoslovakia, third. The men's team standings were U.S.S.R., first; Czechoslovakia, second; and Bulgaria, third. The winning women's teams were Czechoslovakia, first; U.S.S.R., second; and France, third. Among the women, Monique Gallimard, of France, was World Accuracy Champion; and Zoubova, of U.S.S.R., was World Style Champion.

VI. Orange, Massachusetts, U.S.A., 1962

Twenty-five nations were represented, and 133 competitors included 35 women. Americans took four gold, one silver, and two bronze medals. Muriel Simbro and Jim Arender became Overall World Champions; the American women took first place in team accuracy, and the men placed second in team accuracy. Overall winners were (men) Jim Arender, U.S.A., first; Vaclav Klima, Czechoslovakia, second; and Dick Fortenberry, U.S.A., third; and (women) Muriel Simbro, U.S.A., first; Dagmar Kuldova, Czechoslovakia, second; and Nona Pond, U.S.A., third. The men's accuracy championship from 1,000 meters was won by Gerard Traves of France; Loy Brydon, U.S.A., was second, and Dick Fortenberry was third. (The accuracy event from 1,500 meters was not completed.) The men's style championship was won by Evgenja Tkatchenko of U.S.S.R. In the women's division, Dagmar Kuldova, Czechoslovakia, won first place in accuracy from 1,000 meters; Muriel Simbro, U.S.A., placed first in accuracy from 1,500 meters

(Nona Pond, U.S.A., was third); and Maria Stancikova, Czechoslovakia, was Women's Style Champion. The men's team standings in accuracy were Czechoslovakia, first; U.S.A., second; and U.S.S.R., third. The women's team accuracy standings were U.S.A., first; Czechoslovakia, second; and Poland, third.

VII. Leutkirch, West Germany, 1964

The 170 competitors, including 39 women, represented 31 nations. Dick Fortenberry succeeded Jim Arender as Men's World Champion; and Tee Taylor, also an American, became both Women's World Champion and Women's Style Champion. (Maxine Hartman, U.S.A., placed third in women's style.) Following Fortenberry in the men's overall rankings were Vaclav Klima, Czechoslovakia, second; and Pierre Arrassus, France, third. Placing after Tee Taylor in the women's overall standings were Woinova, U.S.S.R., second; and Bera, France, third. The 1,000-meter precision accuracy title in the men's division was won by Schall, East Germany. Klima, of Czechoslovakia, won the 1,500-meter precision accuracy event, with Fortenberry, U.S.A., placing second. The Men's Style Champion was Tkatchenko, of U.S.S.R. The men's team accuracy standings were U.S.S.R., first; Czechoslovakia, second; and U.S.A., third. The women's precision accuracy title from 1,000 meters was won by Valentina Seliverstova, of U.S.S.R. (The women's precision accuracy event from 1,500 meters was not completed.) The women's team accuracy standings were East Germany, first; Bulgaria, second, and U.S.A., third. The final national standings were (men) Czechoslovakia, first; U.S.S.R., second, and U.S.A., third; and (women) U.S.A., first; East Germany, second; and U.S.S.R., third.

VIII. Leipzig, East Germany, 1966

Eighteen nations sent 109 competitors, including 36 women.

The United States did not compete. U.S.S.R. swept the overall standings in both men's and women's divisions. Of the men, the winners were Krestjannikov, first; Gurnij, second; and Tkatchenko, third. The women's ranking was Jeremina, first; Kostina, second; and Woinova, third. The World Accuracy Champions were (men) Gerhardt, of East Germany; and (women) Jeremina, U.S.S.R. The World Style Champions were (men) Krestjannikov, U.S.S.R.; and (women) Woinova, U.S.S.R. In the men's team accuracy, U.S.S.R. placed first; Canada, second (their first medal in the World Parachuting Championships); and Czechoslovakia, third. In the women's team accuracy, the winners were U.S.S.R., first; Hungary, second; and Czechoslovakia, third. The national standings were (men) U.S.S.R., first; Czechoslovakia, second; and Canada, third; and (women) U.S.S.R., first; Czechoslovakia, second; and Hungary, third.

IX. Graz, Austria, 1968

There were 182 competitors, including 53 women, representing 26 nations. The overall standings were (men) Tkatchenko, U.S.S.R., first; Popov, Bulgaria, second; and Ligocki, Poland, third; (women) Woinova, U.S.S.R., first; Morositcheva, U.S.S.R., second; and Anne Zurcher, U.S.A., third. Team accuracy winners were (men) East Germany, first; U.S.A., second, and Great Britain, third (the first medal in the World Parachuting Championships for the British); (women) Czechoslovakia, first; U.S.S.R., second; and Hungary, third. The accuracy champions were (men) Jaroslav Kalous, Czechoslovakia; and (women) Helena Tomsikova, Czechoslovakia. (Martha Huddleston, U.S.A., was second; and Anne Zurcher, U.S.A., was third). The men's style champion was Vladimir Gurnij, U.S.S.R. Tatjana Woinova, U.S.S.R., placed first in women's style, and Susie Joerns, U.S.A., tied for second. The national standings were (men) U.S.A., first; U.S.S.R., second; and East Germany, third; and (women) U.S.S.R., first; U.S.A., second; and Czechoslovakia, third.

X. Bled, Yugoslavia, 1970

Twenty-eight nations competed, with 54 women among the 183 competitors. Don Rice, U.S.A. became the men's World Accuracy Champion, with Zarybnicka of Czechoslovakia winning that title in the women's division. Jacmenev, U.S.S.R., took the world style championship for men; and his countrywoman, Zakoretzkaja, took the women's style championship. (Barbara Roquemore, U.S.A., placed third in women's style.) Overall individual standings were (men) Jacmenev, U.S.S.R., first; Pospichal, Czechoslovakia, second; and Sarabanov, U.S.S.R., third; and (women) Baulez, France, first; Zakoretzkaja, U.S.S.R., second; and Carol Brand, Canada, third. Team accuracy standings were (men) Czechoslovakia, first; Yugoslavia, second; and Canada, third; and (women) France, first; U.S.S.R., second; and Bulgaria, third. The national standings were (men) Czechslovakia, first; U.S.S.R., second; and Canada, third; and (women) Czechoslovakia, first; U.S.S.R., second; and Bulgaria, third.

XI. Tahlequah, Oklahoma, U.S.A., 1972

Thirty-one nations were represented with 187 competitors, including 42 women. The Absolute World Champion (men) was Clayton Schoepple, U.S.A.; Ossipov, U.S.S.R., was second overall; and Pospichal, Czechoslovakia, placed third. In the women's division, Karkoschka, of East Germany, was Absolute World Champion; Tomsikova, Czechoslovakia, placed second; and Starikova, U.S.S.R., was third. The World Accuracy Champions were (men) Majer, Czechoslovakia, and (women) Dioujova, U.S.S.R. (Gloria Porter, U.S.A., was third.) The World Style Champions were (men) Armaing, France (Clayton Schoepple was third), and (women) Baulez, France (Susie Joerns, U.S.A., was second.) The men's team accuracy winners were Switzerland, first; U.S.S.R., second; and Czechoslovakia, third. The women's team accuracy winners were Bulgaria, first; Czechoslovakia, second; and East Germany, third. The national standings were (men) U.S.S.R., first; U.S.A., second; and Czechoslovakia, third; and (women) U.S.S.R., first; East Germany, second; and Czechoslovakia, third.

XII. Szolnok, Hungary, 1974

Thirty nations competed, with 221 competitors, including 70 women. The Absolute World Champion (men) was Nikolai Usmajev, U.S.S.R.; Anatolij Oszipov, U.S.S.R., was second; and Vaclav Hynek, Czechoslovakia, placed third. The Absolute World Champion (women) was Natalia Szergejeva, U.S.S.R., followed by her countrywomen, Maja Kosztyina, second, and Alekszandra Szvacsko, third. The World Accuracy Champions were (men) Stanislaw Sidor, Poland, and (women) Natalia Mamai, U.S.S.R. The World Style Champions were (men) Jean Claude Armaing, France, and (women) Maja Kosztyina, U.S.S.R. The men's team accuracy winners were Austria, first; East Germany, second; and U.S.A., third. The women's team accuracy winners were East Germany, first; Poland, second, and Bulgaria, third. The national standings were (men) Czechoslovakia, first; U.S.A., second; and East Germany, third; and (women) U.S.S.R., first; East Germany, second; and Bulgaria, third.

Here is a summary of American performance in World Parachuting Championships:

In 1960, Jim Arender was World Style Champion, and Dick Fortenberry placed second overall.

In 1962, Muriel Simbro and Jim Arender were Overall World Champions. Nona Pond placed second overall, and Dick Fortenberry was third overall. Loy Brydon took second, and Dick Fortenberry, third in 1,000-meter accuracy. Muriel Simbro placed first, and Nona Pond, third, in 1,500-meter accuracy. Jim Arender placed second in style. The U.S.A. placed first in women's team accuracy and second in men's team accuracy.

In 1964, Dick Fortenberry and Tee Taylor were Overall World Champions. Tee Taylor was World Style Champion, with Maxine Hartman placing third in style. Dick Fortenberry placed second in 1,500-meter accuracy. The women's team was first in the national standings, and the men's team was third. Both men's and women's teams placed third in team accuracy.

In 1968, Anne Zurcher placed third overall. Susie Joerns tied for second in style. Martha Huddleston was second in accuracy, and Anne Zurcher was third. In the national standings, the men's team placed first and the women's team placed second. In team accuracy, the men placed second.

In 1970, Don Rice was the World Accuracy Champion, and Barbara Roquemore placed third in style.

In 1972, Clayton Schoelpple was Absolute World Champion and placed third in style. Susie Joerns placed second in style, and Gloria Porter, third in accuracy.

In 1974, Jim Lowe and Stan Hicks tied for second in accuracy. Debby Schmidt placed fourth overall and fifth in style. Chuck Collingwood placed seventh in style and tied for fourth in accuracy.

Appendix C
Bibliography

Greenwood, Jim. *Parachuting for Sport.* New York: Sports Car, Ltd., 1962. History of parachuting and early sport parachuting.

Gregory, Howard. *Parachuting's Unforgettable Jumps.* Howard Gregory Associates (P.O. Box 66, La Mirada, California), 1974. A historical view of both airborne and sport parachuting.

Gunby, R. A. *Sport Parachuting.* Denver: Jeppesen and Company, 1972. A basic handbook of sport parachuting.

Keech, Andy. *Skies Call.* Andy Keech (806 Fifteenth Street, N.W., Washington, D.C.), 1974. Outstanding photos by a gifted sport parachuting photographer.

Kittinger, Joseph W., Jr., and Caidin, Martin. *The Long, Lonely Leap.* New York: E. P. Dutton & Co., Inc., 1961. Detailed account of Kittinger's historic jump from 102,800 feet.

Mackersey, Ian. *Into the Silk.* New York: W. W. Norton & Company, Inc., 1958. A story of the Caterpillar Club with descriptions of unusual emergency parachute jumps.

Poynter, Daniel F. *The Parachute Manual.* Parachuting Publications (48 Walker Street, North Quincy, Massachusetts), 1972. A technical treatise on the parachute of special interest to parachute riggers.

Rankin, William H. *The Man Who Rode the Thunder.* (Englewood Cliffs, New Jersey: Prentice-Hall, Inc., 1960). A description of Colonel Rankin's emergency bailout from 50,000 feet into a thunderstorm that kept him in the air for 40 minutes.

Ryan, Charles W. *Jumpmaster's Handbook.* Para-Gear Equipment Company (5138 North Broadway, Chicago, Illinois), 1974. A specialized handbook for Jumpmasters and Jumpmaster-trainees.

Sellick, Bud. *Parachutes and Parachuting.* Englewood Cliffs, New Jersey: Prentice-Hall, Inc., 1971. An illustrated description of modern sport parachuting.

Index